# shopping

shopping

# shopping

GAVIN KRAMER

With thanks to Noriko Nagatome, David Reiss,
Rika Sudo, Hikaru Noguchi and Kazuko Otsuka

Published by
Soho Press, Inc.
853 Broadway
New York, NY 10003

First published in Great Britain in 1998 by
Fourth Estate Limited

Library of Congress
Cataloging-in-Publication Data

Kramer, Gavin.
    Shopping / Gavin Kramer.
        p. cm.
    ISBN 1-56947-189-4 (alk. paper)
        I. Title.
    PR6061.R367 S56 2000
    823'.914—dc21                                99-048517

10 9 8 7 6 5 4 3 2 1

For my parents

# CONTENTS

# PART ONE

# I

THIS IS WHERE WE SPRINKLE IN THE
ATMOSPHERE OF THE TIMES
— DAZAI OSAMU

My colleague Meadowlark was very tall and always uneasy. He never looked over his shoulder but you felt he wanted to. Though he'd done nothing wrong he had about him the aura of a man on the run; a man who expects – at any moment – to be found out.

It was not an ideal trait for a lawyer. It may have been, indeed probably was, bound up with his height. In any gathering for a photograph he'd be the tallest, the others clustered about him as if around a young, gawky oak, or a tethered giraffe. He once told me, broad sombre face tilted down to look me in the eyes, as always earnestly pushing up his spectacles as they slipped down the scarp of his nose, how he dreamed of being short. Of being absorbed, indistinguishable, back into the mass. He wanted to be overlooked. He wanted, just once, to disappear. So they sent him to Japan.

I saw him on his second evening, having already said goodnight to him in the office. He was standing in the street, stranded, lost, too tall for that city, that country. Tokyo was in the grip of its late-evening madness, the pavement people-flooded, a huge unvarying flow which passed with-out curiosity around him. In that gaudy, neon-stained district strange foreigners were a familiar sight. Indeed, on the scale of strangeness, because of his suit, his glasses, his well-tended hair, he barely registered, and then only because of his height.

He was grateful to be rescued. I took him to a sidestreet bar. The clientele were mostly other foreigners, white men in ties. I think that helped to calm him, being back among lumpy, Caucasian men, reassuringly uniform in their suits.

'Sorry. I know I made a sodding fool of myself. But suddenly I just couldn't remember how to get home. I felt, I don't know, paralysed.' He dabbed at his face with a handkerchief. He'd been sweating. He blinked, instinctively pushing up his spectacles even before they'd begun to slide. 'You must think I'm an utter idiot.'

I shook my head.

'Well they must.'

'Who?'

'The Japanese.'

'No. They expect us to be helpless. Sometimes I think they prefer it. Just as some of them don't like it if a foreigner speaks perfect Japanese. It makes them sort of queasy.'

'Well, no danger of that ever happening with me.' He removed a small phrase book from his inside pocket. 'It's impenetrable . . . Getting through the day here. You're always banging your head against some ruddy wall. That's all you're doing. All the time.' He looked around. 'I shouldn't have come, but I didn't want to say no.'

'Why not?'

'I'm thirty-four. I'm not a partner. I thought, well, I thought if I said yes, it would help me. You know. Spend two years in Tokyo. Prove myself, as part of the team. And no distractions. I mean, there's nothing to do here apart from work is there?'

Essentially there are three kinds of young professional expatriates in Tokyo. (We had little or nothing to do with the other types of expats – language teachers and language students mostly, plus a few shaven-headed failures who fancied themselves to be Buddhists. They earned too little to live where we lived or to go to the bars which we patronized. Japanese good-time girls, the 'Yellow Cabs', had no interest in them. There was no cachet for a Yellow Cab to be seen with a bald – by choice – white Buddhist, with someone who probably recited mantras at six in the morning and lived in a block without a lift. We also, of course, had nothing to do with the most despised foreigners of all, the slight, dark-skinned men who worked on building sites and lived maybe a dozen to a room in the backstreets of Shinjuku.) And of the three kinds of young professional expatriates, it was clear to which category Alistair Meadowlark belonged. They were here against their will, condemned to serve in this city at this time because of the vast, unified effort of one hundred and twenty-five million people – in just fifty years – to plug a once bomb-levelled country into the very heart of the worldwide money machine, the glittering merry-go-round of bankers and brokers and dealers and lawyers, the see-saw and endless noise of speculation and finance. The food and the people and the customs and the language and the ceaseless, wearying movement – bodies flowing interminably into and out of trains, into and out of buses, into and out of stations, offices, banks, department stores, across roads, across pavements, darkening and filling every space, making and selling, consuming and accumulating – that was too much for them. They worked with their heads down, somehow surviving in their airborne, air-conditioned flats, and dreamt of home.

The second category were often graduates of this group. They were all men, for women (and white women seemed always oddly out of place among Tokyo's neat black-haired millions) found no sexual edge to their lives here. The indigenous men, though getting taller, smarter, more thoroughly label-conscious with each new generation, nevertheless did nothing for them. But for many of the white men in suits, the local girls, or a certain type, became their great solace, indeed their principal activity outside the office and the bar. Alistair Meadowlark, however, seemed asexual to his core. I had never once seen him even glance with interest let alone intent at the flesh paraded so shamelessly in this district of Tokyo called Roppongi. This was the domain of the Yellow Cab, as American expats some years before had so touchingly dubbed them. The legs displayed were surprisingly long. Their mothers and even more their grandmothers (from a time when thick, short, slightly bow legs were the norm) must be continually amazed at what they had managed to produce. Hair sometimes straight, a dense, dark river, sometimes bobbed, sometimes piled up or frothily permed, pronounced mouths thickly daubed, they passed with expressions of disdain and boredom (for what? for life? for their society and patrimony? for all their dull, hard-working parents?); clinging crop tops were favoured whatever the weather, the skin exposed maddeningly golden, abbreviated skirts flickered, heels were dangerously steep – an unabashed peacock display. I often wondered what middle-aged expatriate wives thought, and feared, as they moved cautiously through this parade of high-cheeked amazons.

I, of course, was a member of the third, most select group. We knew our *tanzen* from our *yukata*, our *Dazai* from our *Mishima*, our *udon* from our *soba* noodles. We knew how to navigate the hot spring resorts and the *ryokan*, the traditional inns. We liked to be seen browsing knowledgeably in Kanda Book Town. We liked to be seen in places where we were the sole white face. For that, we felt, was the only true gauge of authenticity. The most fanatical would walk out of a restaurant if they saw even one pair of non-Japanese eyes on entering, declaring the place immediately to be *just somewhere for tourists*. We competed to augment our knowledge of *kanji*, the characters which stand for whole words, and sneered together when someone like Meadowlark said proudly, I can now recognize the signs for Shibuya. The second one looks like a little Swiss chalet in the rain.

So I wasn't at all surprised when Meadowlark said that time *I mean, there's nothing to do here apart from work. Is there?* But what happened to him later, that did surprise me.

## HIGH ABOVE THE NIGHTLESS CITY

*Ma* is the pause, the space between words, between images. It is that part of the page, of the picture, left untouched, as ineffable white. In Japanese aesthetics, in any composition, whether verbal or visual, this absence is also supposed to be savoured, enjoyed in its own right.

I'd met Meadowlark shortly after I'd first discovered this idea and was wondering whether such notions could be applied to a person. Could one, for example, find meaning in someone's *blank spaces*, in the juxtaposition between what was present in his character and what was quite absent? Certainly Meadowlark appeared to operate on the narrowest conceivable spectrum. A single ink squiggle in an awful lot of white space.

It ensured a simple outlook on life but one which seemed to keep him happy. There was his career: new thinking, new developments in the practice of commercial law, faxed or e-mailed across thousands of miles by our head office back in London, would be studied and absorbed with great and uncritical diligence. It never once occurred to him to say *Oh fuck it, what is it this time what do we have to learn/know/do/undo/not do/omit/include/amend/redraft* now. Every twist of an unpredictable judiciary and legislature was painstakingly mastered by him without complaint. There was his small family: he was an only child and a late one. He had elderly, very respectable parents living in a retirement bungalow near Bournemouth. I sometimes pictured them as two doddery giants, balancing on sticks which would have reached my chin. And there was his respect for tradition: when I'd first visited his flat, a one-bedroom affair in Roppongi – we all had flats in or near Roppongi and its neighbouring district of Minato-ku; the partners got two or three bedrooms with better, more elevated views – I'd seen, framed on one wall, pictures of the Queen and our last but one prime minister.

I would have been less taken aback if I'd found a framed still from *Deep Throat* or *Buttman and Robyn Do Rio*, a video one of the FX dealers I knew liked to use as background footage for his parties. I hadn't realized that anyone still mounted photographs of the eminent and the respected on their walls where any stranger might see, certainly not anyone under fifty.

And I'd tried to imagine that room when I wasn't there. The Queen cool and remote; the last but one prime minister with those hooded eyes of hers that disdained like any fully paid-up Yellow Cab; the two of them watching in silence a half-naked Meadowlark (even Meadowlarks eventually remove their clothes) moving uneasily about his darkened bachelor flat.

So there it was. Career. Family. Duty. All of which he accepted, it seemed, without thought. It was that uncomplicated acceptance which for me constituted *his* unfilled, silent space.

I'd brought him back to his flat after our drink the evening that I rescued him. He lived at the end of an underlit cul-de-sac without pavements, a white stripe painted along either side to demarcate a narrow path for pedestrians. His block was the final building, a narrow frontage, cane furniture resting on fake marble in the lobby, the structure disproportionately tall (like Meadowlark) for its immediate surroundings.

A porter had nodded and called out a polite evening greeting as we entered. Muzak, so faint and yet so unavoidable as to induce the beginnings of nausea, accompanied our ascent in the lift. His flat (like mine, like all the flats I knew) had the drably toned interior of a second-rate international hotel. Everything in the kitchenette was extremely shiny and very new with white, unforgiving surfaces. The small living-room, just like my small living-room, was dominated by an assembly of overblown entertainment technology: a huge television screen, two waist-high speakers, a VCR, a CD player, a sleek amp and tuner, as well as a fax machine and telephone combined, all in matt black. The Japanese love matt black. And it's true, like no other colour it eroticizes technology. When you're lonely, when the world outside is largely asleep if still full of random lights beyond your window, you can stand and survey those immaculate matt black surfaces, so perfect, so compact, and feel a strange welling of satisfaction. I wondered what Meadowlark did with this all-powerful array of entertainment possibilities. He'd never expressed any interest in music. I decided that CNN was probably too American for him. And I couldn't picture him grazing with his remote control through the late-night Japanese channels so rich in empty, jazzy, impenetrable talk (with the occasional bonus flash of a pair of breasts) and brash videos by local bands with quasi-English names. On the other hand, there were no books to be seen on the empty shelves. Perhaps he just sat and communed with his portrait of the Queen.

'Do you really admire her?' I asked, sitting on his sofa, indicating the last but one prime minister's portrait, on that first occasion in his living-room.

'Oh yes.' He nodded. 'Very much.'

'I'd have thought she was far too strident, too hectoring for you.'

'Well, I think she did a lot of good things, important things,' he demurred, somewhat doubtfully I thought. 'My parents are great admirers.' Perhaps he liked her strength of will. Liked to set it up — courtesy of that frame and photograph — against his own weakness. He bent down and picked up a video.

'I rented this. Well, Heather took me across and rented it

for me. She also signed me up . . . It was very kind of her.'

Meadowlark dipped his head and gazed for a while at the video, using both hands to hold it as if it were something easily broken. I couldn't see the title. 'I've never rented a video before.' He looked at me, I thought a little shyly. 'Would you like to watch it? I've some biscuits from home in the kitchen.'

It was *Chariots of Fire*. I vaguely recalled it. Cambridge University. The 1920s. Loose-limbed athletes. Gentlemen and Players. The 100 yards dash. Monocles, stop-watches, very long shorts and dress shirts in the evening. Matters of conscience. The Olympic Games. Derring do . . . The music swirled. As anticipated, men in very long shorts in due course ran in elegant slow motion along a beach. There may have been a sunset backdrop. I think the comforting certainties of that time appealed to Meadowlark. Beside me on the sofa his powerful jaws crunched chocolate digestives, initially at the rate of one every ten minutes, then moving up a gear to one and a bit every five minutes as we approached the climactic final race. The abrupt obliteration of each biscuit between those huge jaws was an uncomfortable reminder of the latent strength residing, like a uranium core, in that vast, if presently placid, body.

After the video had finished, the story's strands braided in a tight concluding knot, all issues resoundingly resolved, I excused myself for a now most pressing pee. Just like my flat, Meadowlark's lavatory boasted a toilet at the very cutting edge, all smooth ivory enamel and ergonomic curves – I imagined how white-coated technicians, zealous researchers, must have crouched around shivering volunteers naked from the waist down, prodding them and measuring, to reach this point – with a remote control the size of a TV's in a holster mounted on the wall, and with as many soft buttons, including several to programme the heated seat and one to lure out the douche which would silently emerge beneath the sitter, a rigid, sinister steel snake. As it sprayed on command, one could not but pay homage to so much intelligence, so much busy white-clad imagination, invested in the disposal of simple human waste. *I have seen the future and it works.* This room must have presented the newly landed Meadowlark with one of his sternest challenges. I knew from experience that raw arrivals could spend long anxious minutes in their host's home as they tried to establish, poring over the slim, many-buttoned remote, how to spirit from sight what indelibly marked them out as perishable flesh.

I went back into the living-room.

Meadowlark was still sitting on his sofa, hunched forward, hands knotted between his knees. He looked up, gestured with his head. 'That's a confusing place, isn't it?'

'Certainly is,' I said, sitting back down in the armchair. 'Nothing's simple anymore.'

I was tired now and wanted to go, but Meadowlark seemed anxious for me to stay longer before he was returned to his four walls and the legion of indifferent lights beyond his window. So out of solidarity, remembering that I'd once been a green newcomer myself, I accepted his offer of a second coffee and sat and listened to him moving clumsily about inside his cramped kitchenette. I noticed, resting flat on a shelf, a photograph album. He must have been a most ungainly child, growing in great irregular spurts, difficult and expensive to clothe. I wondered if he would let me pry.

Meadowlark reappeared, holding our mugs.

'Cheers,' I said.

He settled himself and blew carefully on his drink.

'Are those photos?'

'Mmn?' Looking up.

'Just feeling nosy.'

'No. Sure. If you want to.'

'You're sure?'

'Sure. Sure.'

And then he rose and reached out with his great arms to remove the album from the shelf, covering me with his shadow.

I cradled it. The thing was heavy, solid, bound in a marbled red intended to mimic the appearance and texture of leather. I gingerly turned the endpaper. 'I know I shouldn't.'

'No, no.' Meadowlark, who'd resumed his hunched-forward position on the sofa, politely urged me on to investigate his past; at least that was how it felt to me. I had – I had to recognize – an appetite for such things. Yet he didn't seem to mind. I suppose he was lonely, and for him it was a way to make a friend. And so, as I began to turn the big card pages, their photographs positioned in unimaginative quartets beneath the peel-back sticky plastic, he left the sofa to crouch beside me and explain these oblong clues to his past. I was not particularly comfortable with his cumbersome proximity, but I could hardly, as I snooped on his past, shoo him away.

With Meadowlark as my guide, I examined monochrome shots of a gloomy property in a village outside Birmingham. The kind of house where long floorboards crack of their own accord and the funereal tock tock of a grandfather clock is always audible for want of any more cheerful sound to blanket it. There were a surprising number of these, all peopleless, dating from the nineteen fifties. His father, Meadowlark explained, was an engineer whose fascination for angles and structures had always exceeded his interest in people. Then Meadowlark's debut, swaddled and round-faced in a cot. The expression, even at that age, was unmistakable. It was *our* Meadowlark, trapped in a very small body. There were several of him in his bath, a plump baby hooped and braceleted in fat, and even one of Master Meadowlark astride his potty, grinning inordinately, in heavy training. He was an only child – and a very late one into the bargain – his father, he told me, was old enough to have seen service in Normandy as a second lieutenant in the Royal Engineers. Giant and terse, Meadowlark Senior had been a chilly, unapproachable presence in the mess (I decided, as my imagination began of its own accord to embroider Meadowlark Junior's plainer account), building pontoon bridges (his speciality), orders always intimidatingly laconic, adept with his hands and contemptuous of those who weren't. He'd come home in 1946 to court and wed with an engineer's approach to planning and detail (the woman selected, wooed and married in twelve weeks, a short campaign) before joining a small Midlands engineering company. Four years later he was on the board. Mrs Meadowlark's principal distinguishing feature had been her height, deterring suitors and worrying her parents. She'd been only too happy, therefore, to submit to Second Lieutenant Meadowlark's swift advance, hastily concurring with his dire warnings about the implications for all of Labour's landslide victory of 1945 so as not to appear difficult. And in the summer of 1946 her father, a gentleman farmer and Justice of the Peace, escorted her to the altar of the village church. The vicar had insisted on telling anyone who'd listen that she was the tallest bride he could recall in his forty years of ministry.

Meadowlark should, therefore, have been born in about 1947. His mother then was twenty-two. But her health was poor, she was frequently buried in her bed (they had single beds), and so Mr Meadowlark had had to find other things to occupy his mind – puzzles of engineering, company balance sheets, the Rotary Club, his own ten-year stint as a JP. He was a pessimist by inclination, shaking his head unconvinced when told by Mr Macmillan that they'd never had it so good; he'd rather have heard that they'd never had it so bad, considering as he did such politicians' declarations both shallow and presumptuous, mere hubris, nothing more. He was, after all, a creature of gloomy, wintry houses with grandfather clocks whose steady, melancholic tock tock went unchallenged by other, brighter sounds; he could comprehend the kind of life which such places entailed, having grown up in and then bought just such a home, and what he'd witnessed while assembling his pontoon bridges from Normandy to the Rhine had only served to confirm his own dim view of mankind as innately inclined to folly. He was, above all, an engineer – and non-engineers, he had come to conclude, were deeply illogical people seized by deeply unreal expectations.

So Meadowlark should have been born in 1947, but instead his taciturn father and mild-mannered mother settled for childlessness until, quite unexpectedly, at the age of thirty-eight she conceived and, after eight and a bit months of swollen-bellied disbelief, was prematurely delivered of a very red and solemn baby . . .

We continued.

Now he was an uncomfortable-looking, large-format teenager who, unlike others of his generation, could not remember exactly what he was doing when the BBC first banned 'God Save the Queen' by the Sex Pistols. His whippet-faced and far, far shorter second cousin Malcolm now made his debut in the album. Malcolm appeared, at least on the evidence of the photographs, to have been Meadowlark's near-constant companion even though, Meadowlark confessed, he was never quite able to get to grips with Malcolm's embracing of the punk ideal. It was 1977. Meadowlark, about to turn fifteen, was studying for eight 'O' levels at a very minor public school whose headmaster's traditional relish for the cane had greatly impressed Mr Meadowlark. It was a rugby-playing school and Meadowlark, prematurely gifted by his cruel genes with the body of an adult lock forward, was kept busy – against his private inclination – on churned-up sports fields all over the Midlands, apologetically barging down and trampling boys a third of his size, a ponderous battering ram, eyes generally screwed shut against the flying mud and spittle, driven on by the terrifying yell of the games master, his school's reluctant secret weapon . . . Malcolm, meanwhile, had an ear pierced and experimented in Meadowlark's bedroom (closely watched by an incredulous Meadowlark) with the mild self-mutilation by razor blade of his forearms . . . The Stranglers sang about Hanging Around and Malcolm hung around. The Sex Pistols screamed about Anarchy in the UK and Malcolm went optimistically looking for it in the village, Meadowlark (against his better judgement) dumbly lumbering after him. He was dragged to witness Slaughter & the Dogs, The Buzzcocks and The Damned in raw action ('they really were awfully loud,' commented the contemporary Meadowlark) and had stared, aghast, at a bucking sea of spiky heads while playful, subversive exchanges of spit arced between band and fans. *I belong to the blank generation* sang Malcolm hopefully in Meadowlark's bedroom while downstairs Mrs Meadowlark laid a tablecloth for their tea.

By never going out for two years, something his ageing parents had approved of, Meadowlark had done well enough in his 'A' levels to squeeze into one of Cambridge's newer, concrete and glass colleges. Punk by now was on the wane and it was the New Romantics – doe eyes, inexpertly scabbed with mascara, peeking out through waterfall fringes, much fey preening behind synthesizers – who were taking their place. Meadowlark had avoided their pointy-shoed acolytes among the students and also the tougher, leather-jacketed post-punks with raven haystack hair who boasted loudly in the JCR of summer holidays passed in West Berlin and Amsterdam squats. He opted instead for the clean labour and moral perspiration of early morning rowing on the Cam, placed by his admiring teammates at the very centre of the boat, its self-effacing engine-room. In retrospect, this had represented the peak of his life's graph so far, never since matched, with even talk of a blue, though nothing in the end came of that, Meadowlark finally losing out to an even larger, cornfed American. He wasn't particularly forthcoming on this point, but it was clear his failure had hurt.

After numerous waterborn shots of Meadowlark with fellow crew members, oars proudly erect, their sleek craft, the bank beyond in full bloom, the photographs began to peter out. The last one, quite alone in the centre of the page, showed him standing between his now retired parents, the three heads level with each other, posing in the kempt garden of the bungalow just outside Bournemouth. His white-haired, big-boned mother still looked surprised by all that had happened since Second Lieutenant Meadowlark strode with all his commendable efficiency into her life half a century before. He, the retired engineer, remained deeply forbidding, mouth grimly sealed up, clearly still infuriated by all the foibles and idiocies of non-engineering mankind. Perhaps even now he regretted his failure, despite overseeing most closely Meadowlark's early efforts with Meccano, to make an engineer of him. And that was why (I decided) one gimlet eye, ignoring the camera, was instead glancing down to focus on his son's great clumsy hands where they rested, lightly linked. And did this explain – I wondered – my colleague's already familiar uncertain smile?

It was past midnight as I walked home to my own flat. Even at this time there were still salarymen leaving their offices, candidates for *karoshi*, death by overwork, squeezed dry down the years like toothpaste tubes, clumps of them bowing and separating at street level; others were making for their favoured bars and *mama-sans*, or exiting these to head for the capsule hotels, too impregnated with spirits to contemplate going home, or else their homes were simply too far away and it was better (and cheaper than a taxi) to sleep in the stacked hive of those great high-tech doss-houses for the working man. Shoes removed and exchanged for slippers at the long raised step in the entrance hall (just as at home), they would noisily ascend by lift to their floor before climbing rungs and sliding into spaces little bigger than those for a body in a mortuary. Two flushed and tottering Yellow Cabs, long hair identically permed, each with her own handsome African, barged across my path from a side road, then zigzagged past, shrieking as they tripped or bumped something, some impediment, maybe just each other, behind me. I passed the bright red lantern and slatted sliding door with tripartite entrance flap of a *yakitori-ya*, its scent of grilled meats deeply beguiling, then slipped into my shortcut, an underlit alleyway, the perspective suddenly altering, small, darkened, high-walled houses pressing together, my route forested with flypostered telegraph poles bearing a cat's cradle of wires. At the end of the alleyway, under a railway bridge, the last of the fortune tellers was folding up his fishing stool, about to board his bicycle. I continued though this quiet pocket of grubby family homes, then I was once more alongside a highway streaked by headlights, snaggle-lined by concrete buildings, the illuminated lobby of my apartment block visible ahead. Three schoolboys in their black Prussian jackets slouched past me, trailing satchels. Their heads were shorn to a military stubble, indicating they were members of the baseball team. They would have been to school, then on to *juku*, the night-time crammer, and after that would have aimlessly drifted, dawdling in cheap cafés and games arcades, too tired to do anything so decisive as going home. I'd often watched their contemporaries, the boys with their upright Teutonic collars, the girls in their sailor-like uniforms, sleeping, heads lolling, on late-night underground trains, sleeping like old people when barely twelve, fourteen years into their lives. There was so much to be learned, absorbed. And they'd only just begun. There were too many words, too much information. My own head, as if in sympathy, was also hurting now. As I pressed the entry keys, bathed in my building's fluorescence, I momentarily turned my head, trying to guess which out of a million brightly scattered candidates might be my lonely colleague's window.

# 2

## ACQUIRING A SHADOW

About that time I was cultivating an interest in Dazai
Osamu.

Of course, I was always careful to say *Dazai*, then *Osamu*,
never the other way round, so as to leave no listener in any
doubt about my familiarity with yet one more Japanese
convention, the placing of the surname first.

Dazai (aside from writing) had drunk to excess, whored
vigorously, pawned, borrowed, begged, stolen, partaken of
drugs, postured like a true *poète maudit*, brought shame on
his family and finally, after four failed suicide attempts,
succeeded in drowning himself in the Tamagawa Canal in
Tokyo in 1948, a death shared by his mistress. He had
displayed the epic selfishness of the true decadent and
Byronic hero and I was (or believed myself to be) fascinated
by the dirty glamour of it all. I had even put up his
photograph on the wall of my flat – the famous one of him
in Western clothes smilingly balancing on a stool in a Ginza
bar – knowing it would cause visiting Western colleagues
to look at it askance and perhaps even help me to acquire
a certain mystery by proxy in their eyes.

Indeed there were many times when, sitting in my office,
surrounded by paper, his alternative, highly idiosyncratic

approach to life seemed altogether preferable, more vital, a series of fearful and flamboyant leaps over abysses half of his own digging (his family, after all, had money, were landowners); nor was it surprising that the more literate among the resentfully regimented young fifty years on, the part-time rebels and weekend dropouts slouching around Shinjuku and Shibuya or ostentatiously sulking in Yoyogi Park idolized (and idealized) him. It was one of their ways of acquiring a shadow.

## BUNJI

The year before I'd made a dapper anglophile friend called Bunji, an impecunious student of traditional architecture. Bunji dressed and behaved like a Japanese young fogey: not for him Italian labels from minimalist stores or shrink-wrapped CDs bought on one of the huge booming floors of Tower Records in Omotesando Avenue. Instead he preferred to collect dusty 45s and favoured corduroy trousers, second-hand waistcoats and tweed jackets cupped with leather elbow pads. I had never seen him go anywhere without his silver-topped walking stick, discovered in an antique shop in Yokohama.

His round black-framed spectacles were another source of pride. They too had been salvaged from an antique shop, this time in Takayama, where he'd taken me the previous winter. We'd gone by bullet train to Nagoya, then boarded a local line for the vertiginous crawl up into the mountains, the Japanese Alps. On either side as we ascended, where the streams hadn't frozen, furious water gushed solid as glass.

We'd discovered the shop the next day, little better than an old garage, while making a steep climb on foot up from the city to view the hand-carved wooden monsters perched like totems on one of the surrounding hills. Muffled against the cold, for a while we admired these spectacular demons, housed in their outsized sentry boxes. Their mouths grimaced twenty feet above us. Then we headed back to sift the antiques for surprises.

The shop's interior was a simple affair, the wares heaped on plywood shelves and an enormous table around which customers had to edge their way. On one side was a glass-topped partition looking through to a grubby adjoining room. This was filled by a king-sized bed containing an ancient woman, complexion like cracked mud, who lay motionless beneath a thick crust of blankets; her shrunken head, marginally raised by a pillow, grimly monitored the customers as they browsed in her store.

I was particularly fascinated, amongst all this musty bric-à-brac, by the curling sheaves of old documents, roughly stacked in the centre of the table. Densely printed, yellowing and mysterious, they dated – according to Bunji – from before the Second World War, and to me their beautiful characters spoke (without being understood) of the 1930s, the era of militarism and the Co-Prosperity Sphere of Greater East Asia, millions of men on the dusty march in China, that hysterical union of Bushido values with the Industrial Revolution. It was impossible not to be momentarily entranced by the sheer scale of it all, this imperial undertaking ... the sliding paper screens, tatami floors, kneeling conspirators, pale pink glint of cherry blossom, the steady xylophonic tinkle of wind chimes suspended from overhanging wooden eaves, turning, agitated by the breeze, the night-time burnishing and oiling of officers' swords, those vast apocalyptic confrontations of armies caught forever on black and white newsreels in the hazed limitless distances of the Middle Kingdom, before one abruptly remembered that if it all came together at one symbolic point, then it was with a baby skewered on a Japanese bayonet.

Bunji, however, didn't share my reaction to the documents. To him they were just the toilings of dull bureaucrats from some dust-clogged provincial office. The spectacles, however, were a different matter. Upon finding them he waved the glasses at me excitedly. 'Like my grandpapa. Like my grandpapa.' Then he pulled off his own pair, oblong steel things, so he could squint at me through the round and lens-less frames. Momentarily frozen, all that was missing to pull him back through time to the monochrome era of General Tojo was the sepia tinting of his skin.

I thought my friend might intrigue Meadowlark, so I decided to introduce them. Our intention was to visit the Tamagawa Canal. I'd brought with me my camera and a translation of Dazai's last completed novel.

Prior to Bunji's arrival, I urged Meadowlark not to make himself appear ridiculous by attempting a bow on meeting him. Westerners bowing is always a risible sight, though heads and necks do tend to develop a sympathetic twitch in response to always being bowed *at*. It is, after all, a subtle business, full of finely graded distinctions dependent on the relative status of bower and bowee. And if a Westerner bowing was ridiculous, then the gangling Meadowlark horizontal at the waist would be the most absurd sight of all – though it took a while to convince a sceptical

Meadowlark of this. He kept insisting he was keen to 'give it a go'. But I think the huge hand which he thrust forward instead, accompanied by a rather goofy, tooth-rich grin, somewhat daunted my good friend Bunji, especially as Meadowlark seemed reluctant to release him, insistently pumping the commandeered arm. The afternoon never fully recovered from this awkward start.

'I lost my shortbread,' Bunji now began complaining to me in English. A perennial victim of Tokyo's prices, he'd chanced on some unexpectedly cheap Scottish shortbread – imported, the genuine thing – but had then left it on the train. 'All gone. What a waste. Damn damn damn.' He paused to adjust, quite unnecessarily, his tie. It was Meadowlark's presence, I realized, which was making him fidget. He eyed Meadowlark. I could tell he was distrustful of my colleague's size. 'So,' he suddenly thrust at the other man, his narrow face uptilted as we walked so he could the better inspect the new arrival, 'where are you from in England?'

'Well,' said Meadowlark, after some thought, 'the nearest well-known city is Birmingham.'

'I like Devon and Cornwall,' said Bunji, I thought accusingly. 'And Oxford. And York. And Windsor. And Bath too. Windsor, I think, is best for High Tea. It's impossible to find proper High Tea in Tokyo. And the cucumber sandwiches are a disaster. We should start,' he peremptorily added to me, banging his cane. 'Though personally' – this was for Meadowlark's edification – 'I prefer poetry to the novel. Do you like Walter de la Mare?'

'I don't know,' said Meadowlark. Each new remark from Bunji seemed to catch him like a punch on the chin. And, like a boxer with a glass jaw and no defensive guile, he seemed unable to recover his balance.

' *"Is there anybody there?" said the Traveller, knocking on the moonlit door,'* Bunji began to intone. ' *"Is there anybody there?"* ' There was a sheen to his cheekbones as his narrow lips emphasized each syllable in turn. ' *"Tell them I came,"* ' Bunji continued passionately, ' *"and no one answered. That I kept my word."* '

'Walter de la Mare is big in Japan,' I assured Meadowlark.

'Is he?'

Bunji laughed. 'Of course not, of course not. There is probably only me and a couple of dodos at Tokyo University English Department. I'm also very interested in Ivy Compton-Burnett,' he continued, raising his cane. 'But now we must go and look for Mr Dazai's ghost to satisfy our too curious friend here. Did you know he became quite paranoid at the end? All that drink and those floozies, and no Akutagawa prize. The vanity of the man. His self-obsession. I find it all most comical. He also attacked our literary establishment in a big way. *Thus Have I Heard* was his great angry cry. He hated them and they loathed him . . . But are we the right people to find his spirit?'

We set off along the canal. Delicate tree shadows patterned our bodies and the water.

'So why did this fellow do the awful deed?' Meadowlark asked as he shambled along between us.

I said nothing. Bunji simply drove forward dismissively with his cane.

We paused by the grassy bank and took photographs of each other. I had no sense of the dead man.

It was now very quiet.

I studied Bunji and Meadowlark, framed by the camera's viewfinder, as they stood side by side, each clearly conscious of the comic disparity in height. They obediently waited for me. The dandy and aesthete with General Tojo's glasses (and, I thought, the hint of a sneer) and the great trunk of public school rectitude beside him, shaping with his lips that habitual uncertain smile. I was reminded – quite suddenly – of the famous end to Dazai's most famous story. Facing Mount Fuji, its pristine, snow-helmeted peak, the narrator is asked by two laughing young women in red winter overcoats, daytrippers from Tokyo, to take their photograph. He accepts their camera. They pose, suddenly very serious, the great mountain rising luminously behind them.

Initially he intends to do as they ask. But then, at the last moment, abruptly tiring of it all, of humanity I suppose, he moves the lens, ousting them from the frame, filling the viewfinder with just Mount Fuji, only Mount Fuji, its peak, the sky, while the girls, unaware, still rigidly, innocently pose.

He returns the camera. They are grateful. It is a shot the two young women expect to treasure. Eager to develop it, they turn and head home to their life in Tokyo.

# 3

## WHITE MEN IN SUITS

White men in suits, and white men who've just shed their suits, as well as the occasional group of US servicemen bulging out of off-duty clothes, cruise the bars and clubs of Roppongi come Friday and Saturday night. The central thoroughfare is always gaudy with lights. White girls – from Russia, from Poland, from Australia and the States – dawdle on the wide pavement in dirty cream stiletto heels, model-tall and model-thin, sowing flyers while they talk, bored, amongst themselves. They are trying to coax bespectacled Japanese salarymen, over whom they tower, into hostess bars manned by that terrifying mystery, Caucasian Woman. Tiny red and yellow bulbs pulse around doorways. Beyond them are dancefloors already jammed with flesh. An old, bent Japanese woman shuffles past wearing a white surgical mask. Japanese boys in tight jeans and baggy combat trousers gashed with zips, studs bolted into ears and nostrils, pass singly or in pairs and trios, their hair's natural anthracite now a spiky, urinous yellow or orange, while many of the local girls display a predilection for autumnal auburn or honey-brown, sometimes for red, even metallic blonde.

Two delicate dolls serenely crossed our path wearing split skirts, fifties heels and identical stiff replicas of Marilyn

Monroe's hair. Jaded though we were, even Meadowlark and I had to stop and stare as they passed in tandem, a twin, scaled-down homage to the dead actress. I wondered at all the painstaking preparation that lay behind this troubling sight, the hours they must have spent sitting side by side in some smart salon in Shibuya-ku while their hair was turned against its natural self. Heaped up, fixed, transmuted to the colour of brilliant vanilla ice-cream. I also knew, as micro-skirted night-time girls briskly passed, that these trans-formations didn't occur only on the surface. Under tight Lycra tops and lacy brassières even nipples might undergo a metamorphosis, delicately coloured from indigenous brown to Caucasian pink. I had no idea why their hierarchy of aesthetic values should privilege the pink nipple. My own had never been a particular source of racial pride. But magazines and pharmacists happily propagated the means (some kind of powder or colouring stick) for raising them to the shining summit of pectoral perfection.

'Did you know,' I said to Meadowlark, 'that some of them colour their nipples?' Meadowlark was too embarrassed to reply.

Yet he'd asked me to take him out. Otherwise I would have been far from that place, possibly with Bunji, flexing my vocabulary and more advanced conjugations some-where where the English language and Caucasian faces were unknown.

I led Meadowlark into a bar. We found a table, which wasn't easy, tucking ourselves into a corner. I ordered bottled beers from the waiter. While I did so, two Japanese girls seated themselves at the neighbouring table. They chose to sit side by side on the banquette rather than face each other. It seemed like an invitation – to anyone who dared. I wondered if, under their shrink-wrap tops, there were two sets of Caucasianized nipples.

One of the girls had had her hair tightly cropped, dyed a particularly leprous yellow. I was reminded of reading once of some professional punk who'd declared he wished his hair to be *a clenched fist*. This was a clenched fist. Yet her features were classical, the nose narrow and slightly curved, her eyes two clear almonds, the mouth small and very red. It was a face from an eighteenth-century woodblock print, a courtesan of the floating world. That was what her ancestors had given her, passing down the genes which made that deathly pale face possible from the wooden houses of old Edo to this music-pulverized bar. I doubted however that eighteenth-century prints were much to her taste. She would like bands like Nirvana, Hole, Yellow Monkey, Smashing Pumpkins, heavy electronic noise like that now coursing thickly through the bar and to which she was nodding her head, nodding it in rapt silence, perhaps also moving her feet on their thick platforms, not speaking to her companion, her less fortunate compatriot, who had not been bequeathed a face from an Utamaro print, her nose somewhat squashed and Asiatic, her mouth large, sultry in a very twentieth-century way which would not have won ardent courtier admirers in the Edo period of wooden houses, but which was likely to do altogether better by her in the here and now which, after all, was all that mattered. Her hair was very long, the colour of copper, the sheen of her skin also copper. When she stood to shrug off her jacket, I saw how tall, how exquisitely slender she was. Briefly she spoke to her friend, but without looking at her. Nor did yellow hair turn her head. Instead their gaze dwelt blankly, without apparent interest, on the white male bodies squashed together at the bar.

I now asked the one with copper hair (in Japanese) if she spoke English. She turned. Her thin eyes took me in. I knew I was being rapidly assessed. Ticks and crosses were being placed against a mental checklist. Then she looked at my companion. Meadowlark. I'm sure I saw her eyes perceptibly widen.

Meadowlark was staring at her, quite brazenly. And, despite herself, desperately *uncool* though she must know it to be, she stared back. Not that it was necessary to stare particularly long – or hard – to know that this hulking, clumsy *gaijin*, this foreigner, did not listen to Nirvana, Hole, Yellow Monkey or Smashing Pumpkins, let alone sing knowledgeably along, still less gyrate his torso, while seated, to their particular beat. Now, emboldened by her attention (the other one, the woodblock print with the yellow clenched-fist hair, was still looking towards the bar), Meadowlark spoke the only Japanese words he knew potentially relevant to the time and situation. '*Konban wa.*' Good evening.

I was impressed. I don't know if she was, but still she eventually – I felt reluctantly – replied. '*Konban wa.*'

Then Meadowlark leant across me. I was temporarily crushed. He hadn't had time to get drunk, even tipsy, however low his tolerance – but still he seemed to be prickling with unaccustomed excitement. He was sticking out his vast hand; it hovered inches from her nose. Probably no one had ever tried to shake hands with her in a bar before. Indeed, so extraordinary and unexpected was Meadowlark's gesture that her companion's perfect porcelain face had now turned round; she too was observing us.

'We're lawyers from England,' explained Meadowlark jauntily. But his hand remained unaccepted. 'Would you care to join us?' He playfully nudged an elbow into my ribs. Once again I was amazed . . . Lawyer. I rendered this into Japanese for them. *Bengoshi*. Which literally translates as speech-helping-person. We were two speech-helping-persons, each with his own bottle of opened beer. In Japan *bengoshi* (and there are very few of them) are said to be very rich and very cold. Whether it was the promise of our putative wealth or the prospect of our polar coldness, the two young women now obediently moved to join the English speech-helping-persons.

I could sense at once Meadowlark's uncertainty, now he'd achieved what he'd wanted. Still, he was doing his best. His skin had flushed slightly about the temples.

I hurried through the ritual of exchanging names. Little yellow hair with the classical face was called Mamiko. The long, languid one was Tomoko. Then an awkward silence settled upon us. An odd, bumptious smile kept emerging then receding on Meadowlark's face. He shifted his great rump uneasily.

But our new companions said nothing, waiting for us to entertain them. They appeared quite content to remain silent. I now noted a certain hardness in their faces which had previously escaped me. And, looking at them, so expensively prepared for this evening, so thoroughly scented, so scrupulously clean, unlike Meadowlark and myself, I thought, inevitably, of the sadness of Tokyo.

I assumed them both to be OLs, *office ladies*, since it was rare for young women to be permitted to be anything else – though Mamiko's hair suggested she might work somewhere where looser rules applied, a record store perhaps.

The cost of their clothing must have run to hundreds of pounds. Everything they earned was, effectively, on display. Each had a slick, tiny handbag. Tomoko's was black with a gold clasp, Mamiko's a lurid violet, with an avowedly plastic texture. Prada? Armani? Vivienne Westwood, perhaps? I didn't know how to tell. I was more struck by the wilful maddening daintiness of the things. They connoted, to me, an infuriating preciosity. I wanted suddenly to pull them away; to rip them apart. Just for being what they were. But I knew that for each girl those petite, shiny objects were a source of pride, of deep satisfaction. And I was reminded again of Tokyo's stratum of sadness, which is always there: subcutaneous, beneath the skin of everything, despite the brilliance of its surface, the ceaseless movement, the apparent plenitude. I wondered if they also thought about this, the melancholy of new Edo, its origin and meaning. I suddenly wanted to ask them. To know if they felt the same. But, of course, they hadn't joined us to discuss such matters. They hadn't sunk their OL earnings into all this designer wear, these attention-attracting haircuts, in order to go out and debate with us the sadness of their Tokyo.

I also don't think Meadowlark thought much at that time about the strange sadness of Tokyo. He had now begun, laboriously, to talk to them. Their English hadn't proved to be as good as hoped.

'I live with my parents,' said Tomoko.

'I live with my parents,' agreed Mamiko.

'My-parents-are-retired.' Determined to be understood by these delicate flowers, Meadowlark had raised his voice against the music.

The girls looked at each other.

'Retired,' repeated Meadowlark, barely lowering his volume. 'They don't work. Too old.'

The girls nodded. Silence returned to our table.

Meadowlark tried again. 'Have you been to London?'

'Yes,' said Tomoko.

'Yes,' said Mamiko.

'What did you do?' he roared.

'We went shopping.'

'Oh.'

Meadowlark was not an ardent shopper. He hesitated, unsure how to proceed. 'And you saw . . . the sights?'

'Yes, we went sightseeing,' said Tomoko.

'We went Stlingfellow,' added Mamiko.

'Is that a discothèque?' Meadowlark asked.

'It's very cool place,' said Mamiko. 'We went three times. Did you go?'

'No,' conceded Meadowlark, somewhat reluctantly. He wasn't shouting anymore.

Mamiko looked at him carefully. 'Lot of babes.'

'Oh.'

'There are. Go.' Her face was bereft of expression, of any clues.

'We bought tea at Fortnum and Mason,' Tomoko now told him. She had a flatter, more adult voice than Mamiko.

'Really.' Meadowlark brightened at this, three familiar, comfortable words. 'You know the whole shop is By Appointment?'

'No.'

'That means the Queen does her shopping there, you know, picks up her groceries,' he explained rakishly.

'We didn't know.'

'Not personally, of course. I mean, she doesn't turn up

and push a trolley round with Prince Philip.' Meadowlark laughed engagingly.

The girls looked at him, coolly. Meadowlark's laughter subsided. When he laughed with true enthusiasm his whole body gently shook. Now he appeared to be wondering whether his remarks constituted a punishable act of *lèse-majesté*. He scratched for a moment at the side of his nose. Mamiko took out chewing gum.

Meadowlark and I declined the proffered sticks. The two girls began to chew.

'I haven't done much sightseeing since I arrived,' Meadowlark explained.

The girls rolled their gum, waiting for him to elaborate.

'We're just so busy in the office.'

They chewed on, steadily. The strong aroma of mint assailed my nostrils. Both kept their hands in their laps, out of sight.

Meadowlark tried again. It was another weak pitch. 'Where would you recommend?'

The girls weren't sure. 'Seibu department store,' Mamiko said eventually.

'Yes,' Tomoko agreed. 'Very big.'

'Anywhere else?' said Meadowlark, nodding. 'Any good museums?'

'Ginza,' Mamiko offered finally, after a long stretch of thoughtful chewing. When she spoke I glimpsed the shrivelled-up pink of the gum on her tongue. Then she turned and spoke to her friend in Japanese, quite loudly, fearlessly. She knew we wouldn't understand – it was too fast and fluent for me. Meadowlark patiently waited for her high-pitched, querulous sing-song to finish, but it went on for a long time, as if we were no longer there, rich in those peculiar Japanese emphases, a strong, surprisingly confident flow, both girls occasionally nodding their heads to encourage each other. When she'd finished, Mamiko opened up her tiny glossy handbag and looked inside. She started to shuffle, in an odd, slightly jerky way, among its miniature contents, her brow puckering. Tomoko continued to chew, slant eyes once again on the white men in suits at the bar.

From where two of the younger drinkers now came towards us. They were lean, hollow-cheeked. One I recognized. A trader from London called Harvey. The other, slightly shorter, straw-haired, had unknotted his tie. There was a long, irregular stain across the front of his striped shirt. The dying stump of a cigarette smoked weakly between his fingers. Harvey was smiling. Tiny, full-bodied dancers pirouetted in gay lines the full length of his tie. He held an opened bottle of champagne by the neck.

They came up to our table.

'Hi,' said Harvey.

I looked at him.

'Hello, Harvey.' I introduced Meadowlark and the girls.

'Have some champagne, girls,' said Harvey. He poured it into their empty glasses.

'Thank you,' said Tomoko.

'Thank you,' said Mamiko in her higher voice.

They'd been discreetly eyeing the new arrivals, doubtless at work again on their mental checklists. Now they drank the champagne, almost in tandem, holding their glasses very tightly, barely tipping back their heads, barely parting their lips.

'Have some more,' said Harvey.

Chewing coolly, they watched him pour.

Meadowlark, meanwhile, tried to engage Harvey's

colleague in conversation. Behind the bar someone had turned up the music; it was now difficult to hear. Meadowlark's question appeared to be very long and involved and to concern issues of international finance, the interplay, I think he said, of equities and gilts.

'Yeah, whatever,' said Harvey's colleague. He used his heel on his cigarette butt. He was assessing Tomoko and Mamiko. They were what Harvey would've termed Kanto Bitches, Kanto being the region which included Tokyo and its satellite towns. The girls, I knew (and Harvey and his friend also knew), would probably be from one of the drearier and more remote suburbs. Harvey was always looking (or so he'd told me) for what he called THE Kanto Bitch.

He was pouring again. 'Have some more, girls.'

With glacial calm, eyelashes lowered, Tomoko and Mamiko obediently drank.

The bottle was almost empty. 'We want to go to Charlie Brown's,' he told them. 'Why don't you come with us?' The girls listened, attentively I thought. Mamiko continued to chew. 'Come on. It'll be fun. Aaand,' continued Harvey, leaning forward with a wide, avuncular smile, 'you've been drinking our champagne. So you have to come. It's the law. Otherwise that'll be twenty thousand yen.' He laughed. So did his friend.

Tomoko began looking in her purse.

'You need yen?' she said doubtfully.

Mamiko was also peering into her friend's purse. It contained a thick wad of notes.

'No, no, what I mean,' began Harvey, while trading glances with his companion, 'was that we bought the champagne, so you . . . owe us.' Again he gave them his avuncular smile.

I wasn't sure if the girls understood that. Their mouths moved as they worked on their gum. Then Harvey's friend began to dance and sing, joining in with the song crashing its way through the bar, dancing on the spot in a peculiar semi-Scottish style.

I was reminded of that moment when a courting baboon displays. I wondered whether Harvey, as the alpha male, would join in and also display.

The friend ceased his singing and dancing. 'That Charlie Brown's fucking good,' he told the girls.

Tomoko nodded. 'We went week ago.' Mamiko's lurid yellow head also nodded.

Meadowlark intervened. 'I've never been to Charlie Brown's. Is it good fun?' he asked Tomoko.

The traders started to laugh.

'We like Scooby-Doo,' Mamiko said. 'It's hot place.'

Tomoko nodded.

'We'll take you to Charlie Brown's,' Meadowlark offered.

'You won't get in, mate,' said Harvey's colleague.

'Whyever not?'

The traders began to laugh again. 'Come on, girls,' said Harvey. 'We'll grab a cab to Scooby-Doo's.'

The girls looked at each other and spoke quietly in Japanese. I thought they were about to stand, but they didn't.

'Or we could all go to Scooby-Doo's,' Meadowlark persisted.

This time Harvey's friend laughed alone. Then he sang for the second time, his torso and opened palms moving to the roll of his shoulders. It had to be faced that his voice was not without melody.

Harvey meanwhile was once more leaning over the two girls, explaining to them while they silently chewed and listened, 'You see, we feel there's a *moral* obligation here, because of the champagne.'

'But not contractually,' Meadowlark suddenly interposed, looking pleased with himself. Indeed, it seemed he half expected Tomoko and Mamiko to turn and clap at this witty interjection by the English speech-helping-person. I don't think he realized we were losing ground in the battle.

I now took a chance. 'Do you like doughnuts?' I asked Mamiko.

The traders laughed again. They had given champagne, that beverage of princes and financial buccaneers. And we had counter-attacked with doughnuts.

Mamiko briefly eyed me.

'No.'

I think she now knew that English speech-helping-persons were neither very rich nor very cold. Perhaps this was a disappointment.

'Let's go, girls,' said Harvey.

For the first time the quality of his suit, and of his friend's, struck me. Each would have cost four times the price of what Meadowlark and I were wearing. I wondered if this had also registered with Tomoko and Mamiko. They were, after all, shopping girls as much as working girls. Harvey lifted the champagne bottle and tipped what was left into his open mouth.

Tomoko stood up. Meadowlark looked at her beseechingly.

'Surely you aren't leaving,' he said. 'We're going to have doughnuts and go to this Scooby-Doo place.'

'Excuse me,' said the girl in a high, tight voice as she tried to get past his knee. As she brushed his body, I saw her momentarily flinch.

Harvey's friend put an arm around her. She didn't react.

She was used to men smelling of alcohol. Probably it had never occurred to her that men in the evening might smell of anything else. Harvey's friend started to sing into her ear, but with his eyes on us, Meadowlark and me. Mamiko stood up.

'Don't go, Mamiko,' Meadowlark said. I was startled to see him place a thickly knuckled hand on her.

She shuddered. 'Please.' Her voice was girlish, tremulous. For the first time I realized how slight she was. Almost breastless. It was a deeply unhealthy skinniness, just bones and stringy muscle really under those tight, sexualized, attitudinal clothes. A scrawny country girl, that was all. '*Please.*'

'Yes, yes,' said Meadowlark, blinking, surprised, lifting his hand, not knowing where to place it as if suddenly conscious of its clumsy size. She escaped.

The traders, grinning, flanked their booty. Harvey's friend danced and sang one final time.

We watched them leave. Tomoko and Mamiko didn't even turn their heads. They disappeared, between their new escorts, into the forest of bodies by the door. The last things I saw were the copper sheen of Tomoko's hair, so straight and dark and long, and the violet plastic of Mamiko's tiny handbag, her little hand pressed proprietorially to it.

'Looks like we lost,' I said. 'Two nil.'

'Do you think I frightened her?' Meadowlark seemed strangely confused. 'I thought I frightened her. How did I do that?' He was looking at the vast palm of his hand, studying it as if it wasn't in fact part of himself. 'You know, I can't believe I frightened her. But she was, wasn't she? Just then. All of a sudden. She was terrified.'

To the nightclub, of course. Known as Scooby-Doo's. (And which, before that, had been called Bang Bang Bang and before that Boom! Boom! Boom! and, before that, Captain Kirk's Mission, so rapid was the turnover of names and décor, so constant and insatiable the appetite for novelty, the dangling interplanetary craft of Captain Kirk's Starfleet mission packed away, or broken down, in favour of great grungy creations of mock junk, maddened excrescences of wire and steel – subtly mutating as Boom! Boom! Boom! became the more restrained Bang Bang Bang – and which, in their turn, had gone so that Scooby-Doo, fifteen feet high, exultantly reborn in coloured fibreglass, could endlessly leap, throwing his huge doggy shadow over different dancers, different walls as the lighting changed, his bulging doggy eyes and open doggy mouth now surprisingly cynical, lubricious even, no longer the goofy, happy-go-lucky dog detective of my childhood TV memories, though whether because he'd soured with age or the craftsmen had bungled his rebirth I didn't know.) Harvey and friend, all the time, would be making their expectations clear, breathing and brushing and joshing and wheedling in some dark pocket of the club, working to scratch their mark on those two remote porcelain masks, attempting all the time to gauge what impression, what progress they were making while high above them Scooby-Doo slavered and leapt . . . The girls, I knew, would be interested in checking out the *insides* of their privileged, expatriate lives, inspecting the interiors of these *gaijins'* excellently positioned high-rent flats, running their eyes and fingertips over them, trying these mysterious foreign existences out for size, to see if they fitted and how they *felt*, to see whether they could be worn as comfortably as the foreign fashions which they bought . . . but Harvey, I suspected, would harbour more exotic intentions. (For he'd told me, on other occasions, where it pleased him to go.) He would already be thinking of those quiet, low-rise buildings known as *love hotels*, softly lit in mute, dark sidestreets to the back of Shinjuku, behind the lurid scarlet brazier of Kabukicho, lying on its shadow side, or discreetly sited off the major arterials of Ikebukuro and Shibuya, their entrances modest, half concealed by ginkgo trees and a barricade of solid green hedge; with their odd absence of outside windows, they could've been mistaken for the homes of reclusive millionaires – or huge public conveniences – there being no external clues at all to what must be going on inside at any one time between maybe twenty couples, each pair entwined in the privacy of their hired box, oblivious of the other enfolded couples behind the doors along the blank corridors, each room a small sexual space available for rent, carved out of the dense fabric of the city's life. (And after precisely one hour and fifty minutes a disinterested female receptionist will ring the bedside phone to curtly remind those two anonymous bodies that time will be up in ten more minutes and the squealing, half-watched porn video, where a teary, digitalised figleaf at all times decorously masks penis and pudenda, shortly after arrives back at where it started when first switched on, meaning it is time to hurriedly dress and go, unless one wants to be charged for another two hours, time to go back out into the still active, insatiable city.) That was where Harvey would want to take them. Where rooms were priced according to the fantasia played upon their decorative themes, from the basic box with bed to mock traditional (for the traditionally inclined and aficionados of samurai dramas), with its green-tea smell of tatami matting and then on and up by increments of several thousand yen to beds with 'body sonic' (vibrating ever more fiercely as one turned up the volume of the piped adult-oriented rock) and those which rotated round and round and round, no doubt leaving their delicate cargo of naked lovers quite dazed; there was even the opportunity to video one's own performance, though you never knew where copies might end up – a middle-aged salaryman attending an illicit showing of such tapes in some musky crowded basement in Kabukicho was said to have suddenly recognized the fuzzy female form writhing above the sweating stranger, yelping noisily like a dog, giving it her all, as his own wife.

But I didn't tell Meadowlark any of this. I left him to imagine Scooby-Doo's as not dissimilar to a tea dance, only with louder music, where at a responsible hour all those inside quietly departed, unaccompanied, for their own beds.

# 4

## MENS REA

It was about two weeks after our encounter in the bar in Roppongi that Meadowlark was late for work for the first time. We were all surprised, but there was the evidence, incontrovertible: his empty swivel chair in his empty glass-walled room, the PC on his desk still draped in its pale plastic shroud.

I telephoned his flat, but only got the dry click of the answerphone followed by Meadowlark's voice at its most earnest, inviting a message which I didn't leave. Shortly after one of the two partners, Harry Vickers, went into Meadowlark's transparent abode and took out a thick file. Saying nothing, he disappeared into his own room and closed the door. I accessed Meadowlark's diary on my PC. He was supposed to be having a busy morning. Through the glass of my partition I could see the secretary we shared, a bilingual Japanese woman with a US education, taking another call for him. I rang his flat again. And was halfway through his interminable message, dragged out as if no one in the world bar him enjoyed fluency in English, when the receiver, his receiver, was lifted.

'Hello?' I said. I thought I heard someone's breathing before it was hurriedly replaced. I pressed redial.

This time it rang for a long while without any response, whether human or mechanical.

I tried again. The line was engaged. Briefly I listened to its dull, nagging tone.

I couldn't imagine Meadowlark on the phone at this time. Back in England it was three in the morning. And he had no one to call here, apart from us. Yet it remained engaged: certainly, each time I rang – at ten-minute intervals – there came the same remorseless tone. Or perhaps he'd embarked on a series of calls, each time putting down, then picking up just before I attempted to get through. Vickers came out of his room and took Meadowlark's file into Heather's cubicle. She was his favourite among the assistants. Through the glass I could see him perched on the corner of her desk, explaining what he wanted. Meadowlark's own cell, with its empty swivel chair and plastic-shrouded PC, still waiting for Meadowlark's rump and Meadowlark's fingers, was directly opposite them. I telephoned him again. It was still engaged.

I looked up.

Meadowlark, in the very darkest of his many dark, ill-fitting suits, was thundering down the passageway to Vickers's room.

We queued for lunch at a noodle bar, a *ramen-ya*. 'Did he give you a real bollocking?'

I could see that Meadowlark didn't like that word, bollocking.

'Yes,' he conceded eventually as the queue shuffled forward. 'You could say that.'

The manageress poured water for us as we sat down at the counter, then handed us our *oshi bori*, steaming hot napkins. Meadowlark rubbed gratefully, heavily at his face. 'He was worried because of the joint venture. Apparently the client complained about delays in agreeing the contract.'

'Who was in your flat this morning?'

'I'm sorry?'

'Who was using your phone while you were on your way over here?'

'Someone was using my phone?'

'Unless it's started breathing. It was engaged for about an hour.'

Meadowlark had coloured, though it could have been the heat of that place. They were boiling noodles just beyond the counter, the two cooks wreathed in steam. 'It was?'

'Come on.'

'I don't know.' Meadowlark wouldn't turn his head to face me. He hunched over the counter.

'It wasn't Mamiko?'

'Eh?'

'Just kidding.'

'No, there wasn't anyone.' He'd started looking around. 'Where's our orders?'

'Why are you on edge?'

'I'm not on edge.' He ceased craning his upholstered neck; I counted three or four moist pimples. 'Look. I haven't had a very good morning.'

'No.' That was unarguable.

'So I don't need this.'

'All right, all right.'

He attacked the food when it came. You are supposed to slurp the noodles, lowering your mouth to meet them as they're lifted from the soup, but Meadowlark went far beyond mere slurping, hoovering up the streaming stuff into the red and black cavern of his mouth. It was sustenance for that great body, apparently badly needed.

He said nothing while we ate, but after, as we briefly dallied over green tea and the place thinned out, he asked, 'Can I trust you?'

'I hope so,' I said.

'You know, I realize how I'm perceived.'

'I'm sorry?'

'Perceived. *Here*. As dripping wet behind the ears. The Bull in the China Shop.'

'Who said that?'

'Those traders we met were laughing at me. Do you think I didn't notice?'

'Well, they're traders,' I said. 'What do you expect? They're the enemy.'

'No, I'm well aware how I'm perceived.' He at last turned to look at me. Eye to eye. The heat had stretched a refulgent film of sweat across his wide, rutted forehead. 'Does my admiration for the Queen provoke amusement?'

'Well, I really don't know.'

'Do you know people *laugh* because I have her portrait on my wall?'

'Do they?'

'Of course you do. You're a smug so-and-so, aren't you. And I didn't like that friend of yours. He's one also.'

'Which friend?'

'You know. The Jap one.'

I realized he meant Bunji. Bunji of the tweed, the elbow patches and General Tojo's glasses.

'I have,' resumed Meadowlark, shifting direction somewhat and looking away, 'a responsibility to my parents . . .

They're old. They've only got me. I don't want to let them down.'

'No.'

'I musn't let them down.' He picked up his abandoned napkin and absently crumpled it. 'I think I may have.'

'Because you were late this morning?'

Meadowlark glanced at me, began to say one thing, then thought better of it and said, 'No, I think I have.' He paused, then repeated his earlier question. 'Can I trust you?' But before I could answer he continued, 'There's this . . . person, this . . . well, friend.'

'What kind of friend?'

'I think I may be in some sort of trouble.'

'You think?'

'Oh I don't know.' I saw he was becoming angry. I guessed he was someone who boiled slowly. It began somewhere deep in the pit of his stomach.

'Do I know this . . . friend?'

'No . . . No one knows her.' He semi-rotated his empty tea-mug between thumb and forefinger. They were clamped to it with a steel grip. Nothing could have prised them off. 'None of you.'

'What's her name?'

'Rather keep that to myself, I think.'

'Just the first.'

'That's all I know anyway.' He gazed into his drained tea-mug as if its glazed interior might harbour the answer to all his gathering problems.

'She doesn't have her surname on her card.'

'That's unusual.'

'She's an unusual girl,' said Meadowlark gloomily, as if he were still coming to terms with just how unusual. 'I couldn't believe it when she gave me that card. She'd put it together herself, on one of those machines.'

I asked for more tea. The manageress bobbed her acknowledgement, calling out, '*Hai!*'

It was while she was pouring that Meadowlark unexpectedly said, 'Her name's Sachiko.'

'Well, that's a pretty name.'

'Is it?'

'Aren't you going to show me the card?'

'I'm not sure.' Meadowlark looked at his watch. 'I shouldn't even be having lunch.'

'OK, we'll go.'

He took out his wallet. I was expecting him to pull one or two notes from it to pay the hovering manageress, but instead he slid out an oblong piece of orange card. 'Here.'

On one side were several lines of miniature Japanese ideograms (whatever they said, I could tell it wasn't an address), a mobile phone number and, in tiny capitals in the top left-hand corner, four words in English. NICE TO MEET YOU. On the other side the same number appeared again and below it, quite alone, in italicized Roman letters, all lower case, her name –

*sachiko*

As if it had been whispered.

I returned it. 'How did you meet?'

Meadowlark was now taking out crumpled yen from his pocket. He looked down when he finally spoke, evidently embarrassed, and uttered his words so quietly I was quite unable to catch what he said.

'What was that?'

'I said she's sixteen.'

Anything can be bought – immaculately wrapped – in Tokyo: Armani, Versace, Ferre, Gucci, Harrods Scottish Shortbread, Burberry Raincoats, Fortnum & Mason Earl Grey tea, Fendi fur coats, BMWs, tartan skirts, whale flesh, Sarawak teak, Mr Men Souvenir Towels, snapping turtle vibrators, home-use karaoke machines, red bean cakes, Wedgwood and Spode, refurbished Morris Minors for the self-conscious bucker of trends, *The Tale of Genji* in *manga* form, Mortal Kombat III, a Japanese translation of *The Protocols of the Elders of Zion,* inflatable geisha (with human hair), Coles shoes, Häagen-Dazs frozen yoghurt, coffee-table volumes of Helmut Newton and Araki, pocket TVs, Godiva chocolates, the Philippe Starck lemon-squeezer, traditional writing paper, crockery decorated with Peter Rabbits, Suntory whisky, Big Macs, star 'n' stripes Y-fronts, Blue Mountain coffee granules, fragile French lingerie, cosmetics by Clarins and Shiseido – for they know, as we know, that a man is not the sum of his acts, he is the sum of his possessions – Mickey Mouse shoulder bags, Yogi Bear knapsacks, *kotatsu* feet warmers, crotchless panties, English brogues, Konica cameras, Sony Walkmans, Nike runners, J-league soccer annuals, Moët et Chandon, hand-made silk kimonos, teriyaki burgers, green tea-flavoured condoms, Laura Ashley wallpaper, Charles Manson's life story, Thomas the Tank Engine calendars, Valentino handbags, ground rhino horn, alligator shoes, the translated lyrics of Jim Morrison, Impressionist reproductions, vibrating love eggs, Toshiba PCs, the collected works of Basho.

That evening Meadowlark told me how he met Sachiko. He insisted we go to his flat. He was afraid of being overheard.

On entering I scanned the room for traces of her. But there was nothing. The portraits of the Queen and our last but one prime minister still hung there, seemingly unperturbed, whatever they might have seen. His array of matt black entertainment technology still dominated one corner. Outside the window was the city's familiar nightscape, its millions of lights, which can be both a terrifying and a reassuring sight, a reminder of insignificance but also of community. Meadowlark, sitting in his armchair, started to tell me his story.

Feeling lonely (I inferred) he had sat down in the McDonald's in Omotesando Avenue. It was a Saturday, late morning, but Meadowlark was in his suit, having put in two conscientious hours at the office to clear a gathering backlog. He had never been to a McDonald's in England, but here he found their plastic simplicity somehow comforting (I inferred), a release from the highly complex world outside with all its inscrutable bodies and baffling signs. He had begun, experimentally, biting into a double-decker hamburger, trying to locate its taste. When he saw her.

She was sitting alone, perhaps two or three tables away. Very neatly put together, pleasingly compact (I inferred, having yet to see her myself). Her hair that day was worn up, exposing her small pale forehead. She was engrossed in an accounting exercise (or so he, Meadowlark, had inferred), tapping at a pocket calculator the size of a credit card while making brisk but careful notations in a diminutive pink-skinned personal organizer, her *schedule-cho*. She wore a lemon jacket and tight matching skirt. Her mouth was a bright red stripe.

In the watching Meadowlark there arose contradictory impulses and emotions. I suspect what attracted him that day was the image she presented of the miniature business-woman, the doll-sized auditor of books, her intensely black hair twisted up and held by a dark embroidered headband. But in fact all Meadowlark said to me was that he was *struck* by the sight. Rather as one might be struck by the strong colours and clarity of line of a late-medieval devotional painting, perhaps of the Italian school. As if, in a gallery, he'd chanced upon an unfamiliar picture, a small but vivid canvas, and had been transfixed.

Whatever it was, he ceased his eating and followed instead the fingers of her little left hand as they hopped nimbly over the calculator's surface and the fingers of her little right hand, closed around a gold-plated ball-point as it jerked its way down the personal organizer's tiny page.

Meadowlark put down his hamburger. He was now quite possessed (I inferred) by the swirl of these contradictory impulses and emotions. He didn't entirely understand what was happening to him (I also deduced), but something, something unfamiliar – or previously unknown – was opening up inside.

She (ostentatiously, I inferred) ignored him.

It was at about this point that Sachiko's mobile phone began to ring. She lifted up her velvety black Prada handbag and reached inside. Her nails were very long, fluted, a cool grapefruit pink. The device had seemed to Meadowlark oddly outsized when pressed to her face. She talked only briefly. Dismissively. But the McDonald's was almost empty and her voice had reached him quite clearly. He told me he'd been reminded very strongly of watching our supervising partner, Vickers, on the telephone. He'd become (I inferred) excited.

At this stage in the story Meadowlark faltered, then broke off. He was embarrassed. Would he press his face into his hands, and speak through an enclosing bassinet of fingers? I waited.

'Am I doing the right thing?'

'I don't know yet. You haven't told me what you've been doing.'

It was then she'd looked up at him – and asked, in serviceable English, if he'd buy her a milkshake.

'What did you say?'

'I was staggered.'

'So what did you say?'

'What flavour?' he admitted weakly.

'What flavour?'

'It was all I could say. I couldn't believe she'd spoken to me. That I'd heard her right.'

She asked for strawberry.

And so, with a bemused shrug directed at no one in particular, Meadowlark obediently rose. As he left she called him back. 'And one for you,' she added.

And that was how he had ended up seated at her table, covering her with his shadow, cautiously drawing down a strawberry milkshake. At a loss what to say, he'd asked her if she was an accountant. They had had to look the word up in his pocket dictionary. No, she told him, she was a schoolgirl.

The mobile phone rang again. She took the call and had to note down something in her pink-wrapped organizer. The call seemed to be from a friend, as the slightest of smiles appeared on her lips. And then, when the call was over and she'd put away the phone, she'd looked up again at Meadowlark and asked him very sweetly, 'Would you like buy me present?'

And that was how she shortly after came to lead a bewildered Meadowlark (although not by the hand) out into the cacophony of Omotesando Avenue.

He could not quite believe he was accompanying her. It was a heady moment. And with each new development, indeed each time she spoke to him, ordered him, with her girlish yet icily precise little voice, his excitement (I inferred) irrevocably grew.


## HAND IN GLOVE

Though I asked, he wouldn't tell me what he bought her. He elided that part. It must therefore have cost him a lot. Certainly far more than he'd originally intended or expected to pay. He did however confirm that Sachiko knew Omotesando Avenue *very well*. And that, though the distances between the stores and boutiques which they inspected that afternoon were trifling, she insisted, always, on queuing for a taxi.

★

Meadowlark didn't like Japanese taxis. The back door opens and closes by remote control. The driver doesn't even turn his head. A passenger of Meadowlark's build has to dip right down to enter. The back seat is always protected by a stretched white nylon covering, eerie to the touch, with prophylactic antimacassars cut from the same fabric for the front seats; the stonefaced driver, as if also in need of protection, wears white gloves, redolent of endless disinfected corridors. It was the gloves that Meadowlark disliked above all. 'What's he expecting to do? Handle corpses after a crash? The world may not be clean but is it *that unclean?*' Though these weren't remarks which he made to me on that occasion. He said those things, along with many others, much later when his mind and tongue had been freed, loosened up, in ways neither of us then could have imagined.

# 5

## THE CITADEL

The status of nudity has changed in Japan. The old attitude had greatly dismayed the Christian missionaries. Indeed, nakedness had been so commonplace in the Edo period that lovers would even *put on* clothes in order to become aroused. But the Edo period was long ago – consigned to history in 1868 to be precise – and when we entered the *onsen*, the hot spring bath house, we duly separated, Bunji and I going one way, his little sister Yumie and elder sister Naomi the other.

The town of Nikko is surrounded by hot springs, folded in among steep wooded hills. It was November and the sun was powerful enough to merit sunglasses; a month which is so miserable, so drizzly, so *introverted* in England is here a time of untarnished skies and soft breezes. So we'd boarded the train at Asakusa station that weekend, taking the cheaper Tobu line, and had stood all the way to Nikko.

It had been an urban exodus, with thick, orderly queues ranked the entire length of the platform at Asakusa. The travelling crowd had been patient, frictionless, gentle with each other, managing to embark and disembark in the same good humour. They understood frustration – whereas I had fretted and scowled at the first sight of that inconsiderate multitude, resentful of these other bodies impeding my way. But they accepted the necessity for each other, any such feelings apparently conquered, certainly invisible on those mild, phlegmatic surfaces. Yet it had to be there, I was still sure of that, the frustration − a hard, dense knot or tumour − however deep down it was pressed . . .

Behind the low, liquorice-tiled main building, which made me think of a municipal lido, a high wooden fence separated the two enclosures. From the other side I could hear female voices, raised and cheerful.

On our side an unspoken code appeared to prevail, so that whether or not one dangled a hand towel to shield the groin while walking, all displayed the same apparent lordly indifference to the others' body shape and genitals, even mine, bouncing pale pink oddities though they were. I wondered if the women on their side were similarly indifferent, or whether they stole sly, expert glances at each other's jiggling breasts and buttocks.

Bunji's body was surprisingly dark, incrementally graduating from olive to a near mahogany between his thighs. And at first his proximity was inhibiting. I would have preferred his sisters. But there was no prospect of that high timber wall coming down. The women and girls would have scattered screaming, hugging arms to breasts in a way which would have pleased St Francis Xavier. But then a person's body is, ultimately, his final citadel. The last redoubt of self. For him or her to decide, and on what terms, to permit access.

Before going to soak one is expected to wash, and Bunji and I had duly done this: a thorough soaping and scrubbing, squatting down on little stools beside a row of black taps set in a cream-glazed wall, both of us repeatedly filling and tipping small wooden buckets over our heads, the soapy water widening around us on the tiles.

Then Bunji strode confidently out to the open-air pool with its encircling necklace of glistening boulders. I followed.

He'd had to leave his spectacles behind in his locker, so I'd no idea what if anything he could see; perhaps he guided himself by the sound of running water, splashing down from between the rocks into the pectoral-high centre of the pool.

Two or three men already basked there, balancing white folded hand towels on their heads.

Bunji first, and then I slid into the hot water; we lay side by side, gently cushioned by our natural buoyancy from the rocks below, which would occasionally scrape us as we marginally sank and rose. Beyond the *onsen*'s perimeter fence the land rose steeply, impenetrably wooded, an intense, inviolate green.

As I felt myself begin to drift, eyes gently closed, a diffuse blood-orange glow visible through the lids, I unspread my waterlogged hand towel over my upturned face to cool and protect it. We were soft, uncomplicated bodies again, briefly prised from the dry clutch of Tokyo and its rules.

I don't know if I fell asleep, but for a long while only that luminous silence – which enclosed the watery cascade down between the rocks – was audible; not even the segregated female cries reached my ears. Then I really did fall asleep, and presumably dreamed, though my memory of those dreams dissolved at once to nothing, like candy floss in the mouth, when Bunji's foot softly nudged me awake and my eyes opened to see only the whiteness of the damp towel still unfolded across my face.

*

Later we reassembled around the upholstered benches near the entrance turnstiles, Bunji and I and Bunji's two sisters, and sipped soft drinks and milky iced coffee bought in slender cans from the high, bright row of vending machines. Bunji's two sisters were very different. Naomi, the elder, was somewhat plain and serious. She had a degree in political science and taught, I imagined with some severity, at a junior college and also, in the evenings, at a *juku*, a crammer, to make some extra money. His little sister, Yumie, for whom Naomi always paid, was shy and ingenuously cheerful, her mouth always breaking out into whole-hearted smiles, and she was inordinately grateful when I bought her a packet of crisps. She'd listen attentively, head cocked – though quite unable to understand – while Naomi and Bunji talked with me in English, and when I inadvertently knocked my sports bag from the bench, it was she who hurriedly moved to pick it up.

This openness, her excess of unmediated trust – even when dealing with her brother's incomprehensible foreign friend – suddenly troubled me as I thought of those fork-tongued white men in suits who were always waiting, packed together, in the bars of night-time Roppongi, waiting for any opportunity, all with a cold eye for the main chance. Of course, I was sure Naomi (Bunji's parents were both dead) would see to it she never got, unaccompanied, within five miles of that place – and yet I still feared Yumie might one day hear its siren voice calling her; calling across all the dark, neon acres of Tokyo after sunset. She, meanwhile, continued chattering happily, quite unaware that she was now at the centre of my thoughts.

She was wearing a blue and white chequered *yukata*, the

light cotton robe secured by a navy sash knotted at the back, and was demurely naked underneath. None of us had yet changed back into Western clothes. Still preoccupied by this odd, uncentred fear, I found myself thinking historically, looking at her, that slight body, so vulnerable under the loose, patterned cloth, and remembering the men who ruled Japan; not the present technocratic incumbents, but rather their now mistily distant predecessors of the Imperial War Council, thinking of how, not long before the double blows of Hiroshima and Nagasaki, this small band of upright men, in the grip of a terminal lunacy, had resolved to arm the old and the women with sharpened bamboo sticks to confront the Americans then massing offshore. (That is arm what was left to them, already anticipating the coming moment when the last male soldier would throw his life away.)

And I suddenly imagined Yumie in a patched and threadbare *yukata*, together with her dead mother (Bunji once had shown me pictures, small black and white photographs from forty years ago, of his mother as a young woman in a pretty wideskirted nineteen fifties dress, in fact got up just like an American teenager, the frank, narrow-eyed face and hopeful, toothy smile prefiguring so exactly her youngest daughter), suddenly imagined them standing shoulder to shoulder with other women in a phalanx which stretched even to the reddening horizon, rippling across the landscape like the Great Wall of China, an endless human barrier with its outthrust bamboo spears, millions upon millions determinedly clasping the time-honoured weapon of peasants in samurai times, given to them by their own soil, held ready with fierce, anxious grip to repel all foreign invaders.

What were they expected to do? To put aside their

customary habits of self-effacement, the endless bowing, the rigid smiles which concealed pain, all that ancient, inculcated baggage, and to then surge forward, an army of women and adolescent girls screaming shrilly, desperately, wound up to an alien pitch of fury and aggression, sweeping down from hilltops, pouring onward with their trembling staves towards the startled GIs as they came ashore, rolled up the village road in their Jeeps? On Okinawa the Japanese army had ordered the suicide of the entire population to ensure no civilian surrender . . . And I tried to imagine – I had to – Bunji's little sister and dead mother running forward with their ridiculous swaying weapons, like apprentice pole-vaulters, stumbling on regardless over potholed ground for the sake of Emperor and Patrimony, aiming for the hirsute, partly exposed chest of a giant, laughing, hands-on-hips GI, who, still laughing, simply stepped aside.

We changed, then regrouped in the foyer. Yumie had on her cherry-red Puffa jacket, its back printed with English writing (as was the fashion, it was everywhere, this scrambled English, on all manner of clothes, bags, shop fronts). So, once again, I read:

PASSAGE DIVISION
Pilot to Bombarder
Over target in 33½ seconds!

She had been very keen to show it to her brother's authentic English friend and had eagerly turned her back on me so I could read and admire the words when I'd met them at Asakusa station. 'She wants you to translate it,' Bunji had explained. 'She doesn't trust our version' – indicating Naomi

– 'but you, of course, are Real McCoy!'

And Yumie had swung back to face us, proudly grinning, waiting for me to deliver my expert verdict.

On the return journey we were lucky and found seats. Yumie slept, her head safe on her sister's shoulder. Naomi frowned over a translated biography of General de Gaulle. Meanwhile Bunji busily polished his lenses while telling me of his *sensei*'s recent commission to build six houses in the old style in Nara. It was a speculative venture by an ageing stockbroker who'd made his millions and now had dreams of making more while re-engaging with his withered roots. Unfortunately this new client was now proving over-eager to cut corners, especially on the quality of materials, and Bunji's *sensei*, as befitted a fierce purist, was threatening to walk out on the project.

As Bunji became increasingly animated about this *damn stupid broker*, his English deteriorated and eventually I lost the thread of what he was saying. The landscape fleeing past outside – the train brushing 140 mph without a tremor of effort – was now a vast grid of paddy fields, and so I fell to watching this instead, glimpsing the occasional wading rice farmer in traditional straw hat, quite oblivious of us and our train. They were a protected species, ring-fenced by trade barriers, tax breaks, import duties, their old, inherited certainties and values consequently intact. They were as far from Roppongi as it was possible for a person to be.

# 6

What exactly was (or wasn't) transacted between Meadowlark and Sachiko in his very modern flat high up in that
very modern block rising out of the very heart of modern
Tokyo was never vouchsafed to me. The precise nature of
his relationship with her (as the Japanese call it) *secret place*
was something he preferred not to elaborate upon.

But he wanted to introduce us. Perhaps to make what
was illicit *licit* (even though, of course, it would always
stubbornly remain the former) – present her to me much
as he would, in different circumstances, have presented a
large, healthy English girl to his parents in their retirement
bungalow just outside Bournemouth.

And so, one Friday evening after work, we set off
together for Shinjuku. Sachiko, by prior arrangement,
would be waiting for us in a branch of Mister Donut. I
gathered from Meadowlark that their evenings together
often began in one of Mister Donut's many outlets in Tokyo.
'She likes all those sweet things,' he explained.

But, unexpectedly, as we walked away from the office
he proposed a brief detour to a bar. I glanced up at his
face. As I did so it twitched. It was a very localized twitch,
plumb in the softness just below the incline of his

cheekbone. While I was watching it happened again.

'Second thoughts?'

He showed no interest in his beer. His forefinger fidgeted with the small, slimy mound of peanuts in the bowl between us.

'I *can* trust you?' he said. He didn't sound convinced that he could.

'Well, you know what I think.'

'I'm relying on you to be discreet.'

'I know,' I said.

Two empty places on from him along the counter a flushed salaryman had begun an enthusiastic, drunken exchange with one of the barmen. 'I have,' continued Meadowlark, 'a responsibility . . . to my parents.'

'I know. You told me.'

Our salaryman neighbour was calling out for more whisky.

'I don't want to let them down.'

'No.'

He drank a little of his beer.

'They're old . . . They've only got me . . . And sometimes . . .'

His voice tapered off. He drank a little more of his beer. Our salaryman neighbour, face now plum dark, was still engaged in his passionate, whisky-driven disputation with the same barman.

'Shouldn't we be going?' I suggested eventually, my words prodding him out of his private thoughts.

'Yes, yes,' he said hastily, looking up, blinking.

But as it turned out, when we arrived she was eating something savoury – a crumbling pasty pinioned by grease-proof paper between her delicate fingers. I spotted her through the glass before Meadowlark had even said anything. I just *knew.*

## THE PLEASURE ZONE

Inside there was too much brown moulded plastic and not enough light. The shop appeared to be run by young girls in red aprons. Adults were conspicuously absent. The clientele too were largely adolescent girls, clustered at the tables near the door, a handful of self-consciously stroppy teenage boys inserted among them. Only Sachiko sat alone.

She was wearing (she later told me when I asked) a Comme des Garçons jacket, an Agnès B blouse, a pencil skirt by Chanel, and Gucci shoes. I tried to tot up their combined cost but couldn't even begin to guess. Her famous personal organizer was not in evidence but her mobile phone rested on the table. (It had been recharging the morning she took over Meadowlark's line.) She was idly turning through a magazine, clicking over slick, smooth pages decorated with luminous Western models. Unbeknown to her, several tiny but distinct flakes of the crumbled pasty had adhered to her daubed lips. I think it was in her choice of that thick scarlet that she principally betrayed her true age. But when the mobile phone began its irritable bleep and she picked it up, I suddenly saw her as she'd first presented herself to Meadowlark: the precocious pocket-sized businesswoman, fully plugged into the system.

Meadowlark left us alone while he went to the counter. The girls in red aprons, having no one else to serve, congregated together to deal jointly with this potentially problematic foreign man.

Sachiko and I listened to him trying to point out the doughnuts he wanted. 'No, no . . . *hai* . . . *hai* . .'

I studied Sachiko's face. She returned my gaze quite insolently.

'Well,' I said to her. 'I hear you're at school.'

'So,' said Sachiko.

She had small eyes and high eyebrows, slight, dark arches, fine-grained, doubtless soft as velvet pile to the touch. Her nose and face together achieved a formal perfection, but I knew that those eyes would be a disappointment to her. Large eyes, oval eyes, were infinitely more fashionable.

Saving up for that eye operation, are you? I wanted to say, but she might have understood. The full extent of her English was not yet clear. So I just said, 'I hear you've still two years to go.'

'Go?'

'At school.'

'Yes,' she agreed, noncommittally.

'Still,' I said. 'It's important. Your education.'

She said nothing.

'You have nice clothes.'

'I know.'

'Did my friend buy them for you?'

'No.' She gazed back coolly, not a flicker on her smooth face. 'He's too poor.'

'But he's a *bengoshi*.'

'Only the shoes.'

Meadowlark blundered down beside me after placing a loaded tray on the table. 'Here's your doughnut, Sach.'

'I want coffee flavour.'

'Did you? I thought you said apple.'

'No,' said Sachiko testily. 'Please get coffee.'

Meadowlark left us. 'I thought you wanted apple flavour,' I said.

'I changed mind.'

Behind us Meadowlark, voice raised, was trying to negotiate an exchange. Once again the aproned girls clustered together for mutual support while the huge white foreigner made bizarre, inexplicable gestures.

'Why don't you help him?' I said.

She sipped her styrofoam cup of chocolate, then wrinkled her nose. 'Hot.'

'Saving up for that eye operation are you?' I asked.

Ignoring me, she blew on the drink's frothy head.

'Hi.' A winded Meadowlark returned. The apple-filled doughnut, which he'd been unable to repatriate, was still on the plate. Sachiko leaned forward and nimbly, using a scrap of greaseproof paper, removed the coffee one next to it. Her mobile phone started to ring.

She gushed brightly. I gathered she was talking to a girlfriend. She talked at great speed, intermittently nodding her head for her invisible interlocutor, quite oblivious now of the two older watching men.

'It's her best friend,' Meadowlark explained.

'How do you know?'

'Thick as thieves.' He'd already finished his hot chocolate, in half a dozen great nervous gulps. It must have seared his insides. He let her continue, on his face a benign, abstracted expression.

'I hear you bought her the shoes.'

'Well, she chose them.'

'I guessed that. What do you know about shoes?'

The galloping conversation opposite now abruptly finished. The mobile was replaced on the table. Sachiko took out her organizer.

'Watch this,' said Meadowlark. 'She notes down all her appointments.'

Apparently indifferent to being discussed, she dipped her head and did just that.

'Well, did you keep an appointments book when you were her age?'

'No,' I admitted.

'She's very mature, isn't she?'

'If you say so,' I said.

Sachiko softly closed the organizer, having entered her appointment with her best friend.

'I'm in there,' said Meadowlark.

'You are?'

'Of course I am.' He leaned forward. 'Show him today's entry.'

Sachiko paused.

'Can he read Japanese?' she asked suspiciously.

'No, of course not.'

She reopened her personal organizer, turned to a page, then pointed at several faint squiggled characters.

'See, that's me,' said Meadowlark. 'I never did any of that at her age. I was a complete shambles.'

The telephone began to ring again. Sachiko peered at the number displayed. I wondered if she needed glasses. '*Moshi moshi?*' she said cautiously.

This conversation was considerably shorter. After it was over, she opened and flicked through the organizer, then crossed something out. While doing this she muttered in

English – but mainly, it seemed, to herself – 'Ma-jor fuck-up.' She sounded annoyed.

'Did you teach her that?'

'I think she knew this American,' Meadowlark said. 'Picked up some of their . . . idioms.'

The mobile started ringing.

'I'm sorry about this,' said Meadowlark. 'It isn't usually so bad.'

There began what I took to be an argument, between Sachiko and her caller. As this argument was pursued her voice seemed to grow younger, shriller. I gauged from Meadowlark's concomitant expression of concern that he knew – or had a shrewd idea – who this caller was.

'Is it her mum?'

'No. I think it's her father.'

'Past her bedtime, is it?'

Sachiko slammed the phone down.

'Ma-jor fuck-up?' I enquired.

'*STU-PID man.*'

'What did he say?' Meadowlark was worried.

'He's so poor,' she told me furiously. 'I told him. You're so poor.'

'He doesn't know where you are?' Meadowlark continued anxiously.

'He's in bar. He told me, go home. I told him, *you* go home.'

'But he doesn't know where we are?'

'He go home, he go home.' She seemed about to cry. Her eyes had reddened. She wiped at them with the backs of her hands, then picked up her hot chocolate, squinting angrily into its dark, filmy surface. Sipping at it appeared to calm her, but she continued to avoid our eyes.

'She doesn't get on with her father,' said Meadowlark.

'What about her mother?'

'Doesn't mention her much.'

'What are your favourite subjects at school?' I asked.

She wouldn't look up at us. She was still very annoyed.

'She likes home economics,' said Meadowlark. 'Don't you?'

Sachiko blew on her hot chocolate. With a slow, sulky sweep of her pale tongue she cleared congealing froth from her lips.

'And she's started learning French. Say something in French,' Meadowlark urged. 'Go on.'

Sachiko scowled. 'No. Tired.'

'She's a very talented girl,' I assured him.

She now looked up. 'What is *talented*?' I realized that she was, in fact, interested in what was said about her. Meadowlark explained, laboriously.

She seemed satisfied with this explanation. And, as if in response to my compliment, declared prettily, 'I'm so hungry, I could eat a house.'

'Horse,' Meadowlark corrected.

'I said horse.' She didn't like being corrected.

'Sorry,' said Meadowlark. 'I thought you said house. Ears aren't up to it tonight.'

'Because you're *old*,' she reminded him, with all her adolescent emphasis on that final word.

'I've been teaching her some expressions for her English class,' Meadowlark explained.

'Who's older?' Sachiko continued, studying us.

'I am,' said Meadowlark.

'Are you married?' she asked me.

'No.'

'Where you live?'

'In Roppongi. Like him.'

That seemed to satisfy any curiosity she might have about me. She took a shrink-wrapped CD out of her handbag and showed it to Meadowlark. 'I got today. It's SMAP.'

'SMAP,' repeated Meadowlark doubtfully.

'They're band. Boy band. Verrry cute.' This final bit of information was tossed at us like an accusation.

Meadowlark picked up the CD and inspected it. He began looking very closely at the small photographs.

'They're band for young people,' she told me.

'I'll have to listen out for them.'

Meadowlark returned the CD. He looked somewhat crestfallen.

'But I'd have thought you were too grown up for pretty boy bands,' I added.

Sachiko was placing the CD back in her bag. Then she looked up at Meadowlark. 'I want hamburger,' she informed him.

So we moved on, but only to another plastic table near another counter crewed by aproned juveniles.

Meadowlark bought Sachiko a hamburger and milkshake. She picked at the burger with her fingers, pulling away small pieces of bun and meat. Outside the pavement was dense with people. Pleasure-seeking salarymen, released from the office, were heading in their hundreds into the red-light district of Kabukicho.

'So what are your plans?' I asked her. 'Long term.'

'Plans?' Sachiko looked at Meadowlark.

'He means, what do you want to be?'

She thought about this.

'What about *bengoshi*?' I suggested.

She still held a piece of burger between her fingers. She didn't have a ready answer and her expression started to darken. While she hesitated, her fingertips pressed the meat to a paste.

'Or a TV Talent,' I suggested.

'Of course,' she said emphatically, recovering. 'I can be TV Talent, if I want.'

'Who's your favourite TV Talent?'

'Beat Takeshi.'

'Is he sexy?'

'Yes,' she said. 'But he's old.'

She lowered her mouth to draw ruminatively on her milkshake.

'Her telephone hasn't rung for half an hour,' I said to Meadowlark. 'What's going on?'

He kept his eyes on her. I realized he was staring. 'I don't care, as long as it's not her father.'

'Don't you think we bore her?'

'What's he say?' Sachiko asked, putting aside her drink.

'I said you know when you're being talked about.'

'He's being personally offensive,' Meadowlark explained. 'Because that's the kind of person he is.'

'You say too many words,' she complained, unsettled. 'I can't understand.'

Meadowlark tried to touch her, to touch her hand, but she moved it away.

'I thought it was all flowers and chocolates,' I said.

'What he say?'

'He's being stupid again,' said Meadowlark.

She looked at me with renewed interest. 'Always stupid man.'

'That's me.'

'I want cheeseburger.'

'But you haven't finished this one—'Meadowlark began.

'It's cold.'

With a sigh, he rose and headed off to the counter. It was a demonstration, a reassertion of her power, and a reminder to me whose evening this was.

'You've got him well trained,' I said.

She took out her mobile and set about making a call. That was her answer to me; to everything I'd said. She babbled happily; I decided it was to a girlfriend, perhaps the earlier caller. She was using her mother tongue, the mastery of which was her birthright, to exclude both me and the returning Meadowlark. Perhaps it was even her intention to make the point that this was her country, not ours. I turned to Meadowlark.

'Looks like it's just you and me, babe.'

He ignored me. He watched patiently while Sachiko nodded and chattered.

'Is it love?' I asked.

Meadowlark shifted in his seat, but didn't appear to hear.

'He's behind you,' I said softly.

'W-what?'

'I thought I saw her father.'

'Don't say such things.' Now he turned his head to face me, clearly furious. 'It isn't funny, you know.'

The flow of salarymen beyond the smoked plate glass continued unabated into the pleasure quarter of Kabukicho. A proliferation of polyester suits and tan raincoats. Some were already drunk and could only stagger on, arms around each other's shoulders, in incompetent duos and trios. Ahead – for some of them – waited the multifarious delights of the *soaplands*, establishments once known as Turkish Baths until official protests from Ankara necessitated their redesignation, the new name suggesting light, sudsy fun with squealing, pliant partners, or at least partners a good deal less recalcitrant than the world outside. And others in that steady flow might even be hoping that evening to meet a girl like Sachiko, if they could afford her, afford the constant gifts and indulgences required of any dull salaryman hoping to date a bored, covetous but dainty schoolgirl who, unlike him, showered comprehensively twice a day and meticulously tracked the shifting, treacherous currents of urban fashion. I noted among the stream of people several schoolgirls in their sailor-boy uniforms, loose white socks, plain shoes; perhaps one or two were aspirant Sachikos, fellow practitioners of subsidized dating, since I knew that she wasn't, unfortunately, alone.

Meanwhile their role model in front of us was still busy on the phone. She was so neatly put together it truly was a wonder Meadowlark's great bulk didn't crush her.

'What does daddy do?'

Meadowlark wasn't sure. 'Something or other in sales or marketing I think. Smallish company. He's a deputy deputy God knows what. They mostly supply some gadget to Toyota, Honda, one of the big boys. She's never been very clear about it.'

Sachiko concluded her conversation, but only for the phone to immediately ring. Her new caller must have been trying impatiently, all this while, to get through. She answered.

'I think it's her father again.' Meadowlark looked worried.

But her voice, this time, remained at a constant pitch.

She seemed to be in charge of their second conversation, though she said little, steering it with occasional quiet interventions. When it was over she looked at Meadowlark. 'He is drunk.'

'Is that good?'

'He says sorry. I am his only daughter. He is so sorry. He wants his colleagues to see me, because I'm so cute. He has finished his *bottle-keep*. He must buy new one. The *mama-san* says I am very good daughter. He is so sorry.' With a certain grim satisfaction, Sachiko now replaced her phone in her bag. She checked her watch.

'I have appointment.'

'But I thought I could see you tonight,' said Meadowlark.

'No.'

'But I—'

'You have friend here.' She gestured at me. 'Go to bar.'

'Who's this appointment with?'

'My friend.'

'Which friend.'

'Girl,' said Sachiko, looking him directly in the eyes.

'Then we can both come.'

'No. Too old for us.'

'But when can I see you?' Meadowlark persisted.

'Maybe soon.'

'Maybe?'

The businesswoman was packing her things, getting ready to leave.

'It's been a pleasure,' I said.

She ignored me. 'Charmed, I'm sure,' I added. She ignored us both. There was now a certain intensity of expression in her face, suggesting new thoughts, new preoccupations, quite unconnected with us. As if a door had been closed and locked and Meadowlark and his rude, unintelligible friend had both been shut out of her world. He would not be having access to her *secret place* tonight.

And that was the end of my first meeting with Sachiko.

# 7

## WHAT SACHIKO LIKED (1)

She lived (Meadowlark told me) with her family – parents,
younger brother, widowed grandfather – in a cramped flat
on the sixth floor of a tall drab block with wind-whipped
walkways (though Meadowlark had never been within
twenty miles of the place – that was her description) one
hour and thirty minutes by packed train from the centre of
Tokyo. He also told me how she loved to preside over his
anonymous executive flat. Loved to stand and stare from its
window high above the nightless streets, a small, pale face
with ink-black hair, gazing down into the neon heart of
the city, transfixed by the windows rising all around them,
by the pulse of countless lights, a perspective which for her
connoted money and power.

## WHAT SACHIKO LIKED (2)

She also liked (Meadowlark told me) to sing karaoke. She
loved to croon ballads while rolling her eyes and moving
one arm in a yearning, grandiloquent gesture of remem-
brance for lost yesterdays. She loved as well to up the tempo

and duck and weave, yelling as she did so into the tightly clutched microphone – well, that was how she danced, he told me, or tried to dance – and all with the most self-important expression. She really was convinced that she danced well. The teenage girl singers, simpering and almond-eyed, who came and went at regular intervals, enjoying careers of two or three years at most, veterans at nineteen, too old at twenty, were her idols, her mentors. She'd bullied Meadowlark into buying her a portable karaoke machine so she could croon and also rock alone at home in her bedroom with only the mirror for company, checking up on her rhythm and image in its oblong frame, looking forward to her future success in front of screaming fainting schoolgirls, whooping it up in a short, tight skirt, little knees and bare arms really going, before a shuddering sea of split faces and outstretched hands. But unfortunately (he told me) there was an impediment to these carefully polished dreams. Her voice wasn't very good. In fact it was no good at all, and the more she pushed it, the more desperately she tried, the more audible its flaws became. And she knew that, knew it was not nearly good enough for CD and tape, for a year or eighteen months of smoked-glass limousines and miniskirted fame, and that infuriated her. She would sing, sing harder, louder, in the end yelling out her tiny, unsatisfactory lungs into the overwhelmed microphone (Meadowlark, the skinflint, had bought the cheapest model), becoming, as she did so, steadily more furious with her own limitations – almost crimson with impotence.

Meadowlark also told me how she'd had him hire them a two-person box for the evening in a karaoke club, so she could impress him, entrance him, with her singing, her *caressing* of Beatles songs in Japanese as well as the more recent hits of her anorexic heroine, KoKo Wanabe, who, though only nineteen, already had an impressively shrewd grasp of the role of notoriety when engaged in career building, or at least her agent did, and had stretched her slim body – always tastefully, never gynaecologically, naked – across the spacious pages of her own coffee-table book (a book which Sachiko had bought and perused with admiration and approval), the luminous, artfully hazed photographs assisting sales of Ms Wanabe's CDs, the CDs, in reciprocation, helping to shift the stacked-up, shrink-wrapped volumes. And now this CD diva was very publicly dating a rising twenty-two-stone sumo wrestler who'd just made the rank of *ozeki* and won his first *basho*, and was frequently photographed smiling bashfully beside her in his dark robes while his father and trainer grumbled in the press that this was not the kind of girl they wanted their young prodigy to associate with. So Sachiko danced and sang and dreamed of future fame while resentfully attending high school and, in the evenings, *juku* (which her optimistic parents paid for), walking every morning past the elementary school where she'd once played after class until the wholemeal strains of the cor anglais solo from Dvorak's New World Symphony, broadcast late each afternoon, finally prompted the excited children on their way before the closing of the gates. But now she'd grown up, now she understood the world, and was no longer a silly, unthinking infant, of that she was sure. Meanwhile, at her all-girls high school, and much against her will, she'd been press-ganged into playing for the volleyball team and wasn't even allowed to wear her Nike trainers with spirit-levels built into the transparent plastic soles – how she complained to Meadowlark about that, and at inordinate length, reminding him, perhaps, of his own days as an adult-sized lock forward reluctantly trampling down schoolboys in the Midlands mud. So I pictured her playing in a gym full of feminine cries and rubber-soled shrieks, leaping in tandem with a taller teammate to make a well-coached block, hating the ball, angry with that painful projectile which, like the spinster gamesmistress, would never leave her alone to cultivate her true destiny. And I pictured her in the changing room and showers after, joining in – with the knowledge of weary experience – all the girl chat about teen icons and new fashions, already a label veteran, and therefore entitled to advance her own views on the subject most forcefully, impressing and leading the label-innocent among her peers as they towelled their dripping hair and listened attentively until the gamesmistress came in to rudely quieten them down.

# 8

## THE NEW MAN

I noticed how Meadowlark now looked about him when-
ever we walked in the street together with a new appetite;
with an unfamiliar and predatory light in eyes made so
small and remote by the power of his thick lenses. I found
something disturbing in this new enthusiasm.

'Looking at the girls, are you?' I said.

Before, he might have been embarrassed. Now he said,
'Well, they choose to make a display of themselves.'

'But isn't that disloyal to Sachiko?'

High above me, Meadowlark laughed with Olympian
detachment.

'Well why don't you approach one? Why stop at looking?'

He ignored me. He was following with his eyes two
slender OLs in corporate livery (green blazers, conservative
hemlines) coming out of a tea-shop. Through the plate
glass I could see their table being cleared of its fragile china
cups and saucers, leaving two oval dessert plates bearing
the collapsed strawberry ruins of the cream cakes they'd
toyed with and picked at in a suitably ladylike way.

'I don't think they're raunchy enough for you.'

Once again he bestowed on me his Olympian laugh. He
was very pleased with himself. And I knew the reason why

– his possession of Sachiko. He'd even stopped writing (or so he'd told me) to Victoria, a no-nonsense country girl (or so she'd appeared in the photo he'd shown me of her in mud-crusted wellingtons and Barbour jacket and man's check cap) whom he'd taken once or twice to the cinema and once or twice to watch dressage, though I didn't know whether once or twice he'd slid a great arm surreptitiously around her admirably broad shoulders. Poor Victoria. I wondered if she missed him. But she was thirty-three, so how could she have ever hoped to compete with Sachiko, so fresh and unlined, skin so smooth, such a healthy glow. My revivified colleague was even, for the first time, taking pleasure in his height and physique, telling me how Japanese men – so expert usually at feigning polite disinterest – would turn and gaze bemused in their wake as he and Sachiko passed.

We stopped outside the noodle bar where we intended to have lunch. The full menu was recreated in sun-faded plastic models in a six-tier display case at the entrance. Meadowlark wagged confidently with a forefinger at the manageress who came outside. He pointed at one of the reproduction dishes on the top tier. '*Kore o kudasai,*' he declared loudly. I'll have this.

While we were eating, I said, 'Did you give Harry the Sanderson contract?'

Meadowlark paused, his heavily loaded chopsticks in mid-ascent. 'Shit.'

'He won't be very pleased.'

'I know he won't be very pleased.'

'Sanderson's flying in tomorrow from Singapore.'

'Shit.'

'You can borrow my Ikotech file if you like. Use that as a precedent. It's virtually the same deal.'

'I better,' said Meadowlark. 'Thanks,' he added.

His mouth closed over the suspended noodles. His jaw muscles bulged. The act of eating calmed him.

'I met Harvey yesterday,' he now began, resting his chopsticks on the counter. 'Bumped into him at Roppongi station. Told me he's off on a long weekend with six traders. One of them's getting married.'

'That's nice. Local girl?'

'No. English. So it's a stag night, well, stag weekend.'

'Where are they going?'

'Thailand.'

'Bangkok?'

'He didn't say. Actually, he invited me along.'

'Was he being serious?'

'Why not?'

'I thought you thought they laughed at you.'

'I met him by chance recently. In a bar. I was with Sachiko. He was quite civil. If slightly too . . . curious.' Meadowlark picked up his chopsticks.

'Are you going?'

'They're not my sort,' said Meadowlark. 'Harvey's a bit loutish to be honest. Did you know his father's a lorry-driver? I don't mean,' he continued, 'there's anything wrong with that but still, I was surprised.' He paused.

'I didn't know that.'

'Yes. I was surprised.'

He resumed eating.

'So you're not going?'

'No.'

'You might enjoy it.'

'Why should I enjoy it?'

'All those dark, available bodies.'

'Why, have you been there?'

'No.'

'Like to, though, wouldn't you?'

'No.'

'Well, I think you would. Provided you were alone. Provided no one was watching you . . . What about that Dazai fellow of yours. He ever go?'

'No. Thailand was an innocent place then.'

Meadowlark paused to gulp cold water expansively, head thrown back.

'How's Sachiko?'

The glass came down. He reached with his free hand into his inside pocket and took out a mobile phone.

'You've joined the club.'

'I've joined the club.'

'Congratulations.'

He rang her. I waited.

'It's off,' he said, placing his phone on the counter.

'Maybe teacher confiscated it.'

Meadowlark resumed eating, but three more times he broke off to try her. Each time Sachiko's mobile remained silenced. I could see that her unavailability annoyed him, though he wrestled with his features to conceal this. Still, I saw his broad face darken (I think he'd wanted to prove something to me) and he gorged himself instead on the noodles. Finally, he lifted the great bowl and swilled down the murky, noodle-less pond at the bottom, his skin a chilli red from the heat of that place.

We returned to the office. My stray remarks as we walked were ignored. He was still angry. This distancing made him seem even taller. An inaccessible peak, no longer so easily scaled. His face, its dull, unwelcoming expression, made me think of Kabukicho in the late morning, all the fun now just a memory, the windy latticework of passageways largely deserted, scraps of rubbish shifting uneasily like autumn leaves, the light dirty, the pleasure palaces mostly closed, a few bored leather-jacketed men in doorways, the jamb and wall above the steps leading downstairs decorated with smiling photos of the girls allegedly inside, waiting on a row of plastic chairs, the leather jackets desultorily calling out to the occasional male passer-by, but not really caring, hunching over their cigarettes (it's a cold morning), shrill feminine voices crying out these places' wares over unseen loudspeakers placed high above, doubtless making promises of what is in store, what is available, but it's turning into a dreary, overcast day and no one – in truth – is really listening.

# 9

## AT THE FAIR

Bunji's little sister, Yumie, had a best friend, Midori. They were in the same class at high school. Midori's father was a *yakuza*, a mobster (or so Bunji informed me), with a shaggy sheepskin coat and a permed head of tight curls, a hot-house of tattoos spiralling out over his body like a Maori, and a pearl (Bunji assured me, this time dropping his voice) surgically inserted into his penis to enhance its sexual efficacy. His daughter was a quiet, bespectacled girl who liked Jane Austen, but her father – as befitted a senior figure in the Wagamama-gumi – would insist on embarrassing her by turning up at school open days ringed by a *cordon sanitaire* of henchmen in shades. Her mother (Bunji leered) had a great swan tattooed on her back. She'd once – when tipsy in the afternoon – shown it to Yumie, who'd thought the long-necked bird very beautiful and serene.

Beautiful and serene. That description, of all possible descriptions, helped the mind's eye to conjure the image, the outspread snowy creature beneath the bunched-up blouse, garrotted by the flesh-coloured bra strap, etched with the clarity of a woodblock print into the once alabaster but now creased and liver-spotted skin of Midori's mother's back, a back in decline, no longer capable, if it ever was, of retaining her husband's undivided attention – and doubtless he only rarely now drew his tongue down its long dry runnel, preferring instead to climb into his imported black Mercedes Benz with two or three of his cohorts and take his surgically augmented member elsewhere. While his wife cursed in her carpeted bedroom and pointlessly flung a long fluted glass (still full) at her wardrobe of fur and cashmere.

Yet there was no trace of this home life anywhere on Midori's own bespectacled face. It was round, chubby, more Chinese I thought than Japanese, pleasantly bookish, her nose barely raising the surface of her skin, and she chattered happily enough with Yumie, her best and very reliable friend, as we headed off for an evening at the *matsuri*, the festival and fair.

Just beyond the station, rising into the early winter darkness, were two vast parallel walls composed of yellow lanterns, great fat drums of blazing light, each the height of a child, tier upon tier, bold black ideograms stamped down their glowing convex sides. We passed along the broad thorough-fare which they created, drifting with the crowd, dawdling in front of the bright stalls which lined the base of both walls. The girls bought and shared a styrofoam tray of grilled octopus, the tentacles chopped into knobbled segments. Tiny children in dark blue kimonos scampered around us. Bunji led the way. Behind the girls a sulking Meadowlark loomed, less a part of our group than its backdrop, turning down the plump, blackened chunks of octopus which they swung round to cheerfully offer him, expertly pinioned between their chopsticks. At one end of the fair a bandstand had been set up, fringed by strings of globular lanterns which threw down a lychee-like light, and a thickening body of people now circled it, dancing as they moved to the ancient melody struck up by drums and flutes. Many of the male musicians were bare to the midriff, a strip of twisted cloth tied tight around their heads. We paused to admire the dancers' brightly robed progress, here and there the glint of spectacles, as arms snaked in strange, mesmeric patterns, hands extended, sometimes inverted, white-socked feet shod in red-thonged sandals advancing in measured steps, the dancers mostly women, mostly middle-aged or older, some waving circular fans, others bending down to guide the little wrists of a bemused grandchild shuffling forward between their legs. I spotted two or three outsized white men clad in checkered *yukatas* dancing unself-consciously among them, confidently flaunting their knowledge of the correct steps and hand movements, maybe acquired while teaching English in Kyoto or some other traditional town.

'They look ridiculous,' said Meadowlark huffily, watching the white men. Then he pushed me in the small of my back. 'Why don't you join in?' He looked down at Bunji. 'Can you do the moves?'

'Yes,' said Bunji, without turning.

'I think they dance well,' said Midori softly.

'They look ridiculous,' Meadowlark repeated.

We moved on, into the field beyond the walls of elec-trified lanterns. Beside me, Yumie gasped, then pulled at her friend's elbow. She was gazing up at a sign fixed to a high, temporary fence behind which a sullen green marquee had been pitched.

We gathered together to inspect the sign, even Meadow-lark. The drawing on it was crude and unambiguous: three men in Ancient Egyptian profile, all smiling faintly, each with the four stocky legs of a Shetland pony and, obscured by those hirsute shanks, a full, rubbery cow's udder. 'I like this show,' said Bunji. Other people were already going in, a steady flow of the curious.

The girls were reluctant. Yumie clung to the *yakuza's* daughter, making mock, high-pitched sounds of fear. She didn't want to see, but I knew another part of her wanted to. I think I was in that camp also. Midori waited, while her friend held her, with an expression of apparently calm neutrality, although I could tell she was the more reluctant. 'Are they real freaks?' Meadowlark asked.

But Bunji was already striding past the barrier. The girls followed, Yumie still clinging to Midori, still emitting her mock protestations. Meadowlark reflectively rubbed and pressurized his bull's neck, still contemplating the sign. 'It can't be real. No one goes around looking like that.'

We were the last in. Attendants in overalls moved to close the barrier behind us. We forced our way deeper into the marquee's packed interior, looking for the others. Behind us, the tent flap slithered down, blocking off any view of the stalls and lanterns outside. Ahead was a high, deep stage – curtained off behind and on either side – around which respect or caution, rather than the uniformed attendants, had drawn a semicircle of unpeopled grassy space. The attendants were now moving among the crowd, collecting payment and issuing tickets. But we weren't looking at them. Like everyone else around us we were stretching, craning (except for Meadowlark, who had no need to stretch or crane) for a better view of the woman waiting on the stage to welcome us, her faint smile a perfect match for the faint smiles in Ancient Egyptian profile of the horsemen with bursting udders on the sign outside. At first I thought she was an amputee, for her torso seemed to have been placed down flat on the stage like an oversized chess piece. Then I realized that she did indeed have legs, but that these were stretched out directly behind her; it was anatomically impossible, like two flat strips of rubber. Lifeless. But she could not have been feeling any pain, for nothing undermined that steady smile with which she regarded us while we were accosted for notes and coins by the attendants with their perforated ticket rolls.

The woman began to speak, in Japanese. 'What's she saying?' said Meadowlark, though he must have known I wouldn't be able to understand most of it. All I knew for certain was that she'd welcomed us and had expressed her fervent wish that we enjoy the evening ahead. After that it was impenetrable. So while everyone else listened, even the uncomprehending Meadowlark, and the girls and women around us, some in kimonos, clung, prettily open-mouthed, to their boyfriends' or husbands' arms, I fell to studying her face. 'How old d'you think she is?'

'What?' grunted Meadowlark. He was staring intently.

She seemed to me somewhere between forty and forty-five. I'd noticed she'd had her hair done in a style not dissimilar to one of my aunts back in England. I was about to mention this to Meadowlark when he grabbed my shoulder.

'Look.'

The woman was still talking, still patiently explaining, still faintly smiling, but, as if she'd heard his hoarse ejaculation, her head appeared to turn in our direction so as to locate and reprimand the source of this disturbance. But while her neck swivelled her mouth continued speaking, in the same clear, measured way. Perhaps, I thought, it wasn't Meadowlark. Perhaps she was simply making sure that we each had our chance to look right into those rather run-of-the-mill forty- or forty-five-year-old Japanese eyes beneath that hairstyle so uncannily reminiscent of my aunt's and which required (I therefore knew) the best part of a morning or afternoon at the salon to assemble, to be washed and crimped and moulded and so brought to fruition.

'Did you see that?' Meadowlark's hand was no longer on my shoulder; he'd now pushed himself alongside me.

'I was looking at her hair.'

'No, when someone lifted that curtain—'

There was a collective gasp of surprise from the audience, blotting out the rest of Meadowlark's words. Out onto the stage they came. I will never know how they did it. Three men bent double, their backs dangerously hooped as they advanced to the edge of the stage, their necks upright, heads alert, observing us; walking, tiptoeing, on their arms and legs, but those arms and legs, I realized, were in fact the four shaggy, bandy legs of a Shetland pony – no they weren't, they were just arms and legs, horribly, impossibly contorted, the men's necks and heads so stiffly, unpleasantly erect and all bearing, on their bland faces, as promised by the sign, those faint smiles (which are worse than mocking smiles or sour smiles; indeed it seemed, at that moment, there could be no expression more terrible than those faint, smugly ineffable smiles). 'Look,' insisted Meadowlark, as if there was something else we might equally have chosen to do. And now I saw, between those horses' legs – no, arms and legs, just human arms and legs, but so cleverly contorted – *udders*, fat, rubbery teats, albeit hints only, coy glimpses, as if they were shy to admit to those appendages, swollen enough even to be milked. Several girls screamed as they, whatever they were, came right up close, to the very edge of the stage, their raised heads continuing to observe us. What was that oscillating movement bulging and deflating their throats? The cud, they were chewing the cud. I looked at the woman with my aunt's hair who still merely sat there, I thought now with a certain proprietorial pride; her own faint smile remained in place and her head, as before, was swivelling in thoughtful contemplation of this host of open-mouthed voyeurs come to see the freaks, just as they, the freaks, were queuing on the other side of the drawn curtain to see us, I felt sure.

'I can see the girls,' Meadowlark said.

'Are they watching?'

'No. They're hiding their faces.'

'Where are they?'

'This way,' said Meadowlark.

He started to push a path through to them, using his shoulder like the prow of a ship. Around us his progress provoked murmurs of complaint. I followed close in his wake, just as another gasp went up from the audience.

'Who's on now?' I shouted at the back of Meadowlark's head.

'It's not possible,' was all he said. I could feel a restlessness now in the tent. Not only young women were turning to look away, just as others stretched and craned with an overripe fascination, greedy for each new sensation. Then I realized that Bunji was immediately in front of us. He twisted his head to greet me. He was grinning. On the stage there were two children. An interlude? Then I saw they were dwarves. Two oriental dwarves. They appeared mightily pleased with themselves. One was bare-chested – with overdeveloped pectorals – and was flapping something limp and flimsy in the other's face. It was a third arm, a third arm with the consistency and texture of a thick tentacle. Maybe this *was* an interlude, a comic interlude, for the two dwarves were leaping loudly around the stage and shouting gutturally at each other. I also saw that our mistress of ceremonies had gone. Had she been carried off?

The girls were sheltering behind Bunji's back. 'We want to go,' said the *yakuza*'s daughter.

'I'll take them out,' I told Bunji.

And we left him and Meadowlark together.

From the stage I could still hear the combative cries of those argumentative dwarves and the slap slap of the tentacle-arm as it found its target.


We waited outside. Midori had sat down on a bench, Yumie beside her. Yumie's face was flushed.

'Was she frightened?' I said to Midori in English.

'What did he say?' Yumie asked in Japanese.

I told her.

She nodded her head vigorously.

'Were they real?' Midori wondered shyly. 'The men-horse?' She seemed to be smiling.

'I don't know. No, I'm sure they weren't.'

'They looked real . . . I felt bad to stare. I felt sorry for them.'

I knew they couldn't be real, but part of me remained unsure. Yumie suddenly brightened. I looked round. Bunji was coming towards us, still grinning. Meadowlark was not far behind.

'Brilliant,' declared Bunji.

'Eeugh,' insisted Yumie.

'You missed a three-breasted woman,' said Meadowlark. 'In a three-cup bra.' He laughed.

Yumie looked at us quizzically. Bunji translated.

'Oh.' She covered her mouth with her hand, giggling softly, embarrassed but intrigued. 'Impossible,' she added in Japanese in a low voice.

'What did she say?' asked Meadowlark.

'She thinks it's impossible,' I explained.

'Well, they bounced around very realistically,' said Meadowlark, most amused. 'If you ask me.' I noticed he was no longer sulking.

'Have you spoken to Sachiko?'

'Just got through. Seeing her later. Well, quite a lot later.'

'A midnight assignation. Did you tell her where you'd been?'

'Tried to, but she doesn't know the word "freak".'

'He's got to meet his girlfriend later,' I told the others in Japanese.

Yumie was interested. She wanted to know all about Meadowlark's girlfriend.

'Is she pretty?'

'Yes.'

'Is she as big as him?'

Midori covered her mouth to hide her smile.

'No, she's only this size.' I brought my hands close together.

'What's all this jabber-jabber then?' said Meadowlark jauntily.

'I'm telling them about your girlfriend. They're fascinated.'

'My girlfriend,' said Meadowlark (in English), raising one finger. 'Beauti-ful.'

The girls looked at his finger. He thought for a moment, then declared in triumphant Japanese, '*O-ishii!*'

Tasty.

Yumie giggled.

'English?' she said to Meadowlark, her eyes now suddenly quite mischievous. 'Bronde?'

He shook his head. '*Nihonjin.*'

'What does she do?' Midori interrupted quietly.

Meadowlark paused.

'She's a businesswoman,' he said finally. 'She's in . . . business.' Midori translated this for Yumie. The two girls nodded their heads, murmuring in unison ('*mmmmmmn*') as they digested this interesting information.

'Japanese businesswoman,' said Midori. 'Very smart. Travel world. Like man.'

'Well, she doesn't travel that much.' Meadowlark's enthusiasm for this discussion of Sachiko and her qualities now appeared to be waning. Instead he abruptly threw a fraternal arm around Bunji. I was astonished.

'Where next?' he demanded loudly. A startled Bunji broke away. 'Let's go drinking,' he continued, looming darkly over the rest of our little group, his great bulk back-lit by the yellow lanterns.

'We could,' said Bunji. 'Maybe. But my sister must go home soon.'

'Let's go to Roppongi,' said Meadowlark. He was considering, in an oblique, lazy way, the *yakuza*'s daughter. She was still seated on the bench, her bespectacled face mild and impassive. 'Could try and get this one drunk,' he added to Bunji and me. 'Find her a nice trader.' He fell again to palpitating his bull's neck while he spoke, using both hands to press free whatever tension his flesh contained. 'What does Harvey call it? Leg-over-liquor. Told me that's his secret. Knowing a girl's particular leg-over-liquor.' Briefly he laughed. 'Hers'll be a shandy.' He laughed again.

'What does he mean?' Midori asked quietly. 'About me?'

'Come on. Let's go.' Meadowlark was pounding vacant air with his fists, revving himself up. He was impatient. His body's wide shadow, cast by the wall of electric lanterns, covered the girls on the bench. The shadows of his arms, long black stripes, swept back and forth on the grass.

'Is your colleague being rude about my sister's best friend?' Bunji asked me suddenly.

'Doesn't this fellow know what a joke is?' said Meadowlark, still battering away at the air. He seemed now to be all appetite.

'I don't know. Ask him.'

Bunji came up close to Meadowlark. 'You were being rude. Yes?'

'What did he say about me?' The *yakuza*'s daughter spoke softly, but she was interested. Yumie whispered something to her in Japanese.

'What is "leg-over"?' Bunji now asked me, turning his face, head level with Meadowlark's chest.

'Best we don't tell him, I think,' said Meadowlark in a stage whisper, still relentlessly jabbing. He stepped back, uncovering the girls.

'No, don't tell me,' said Bunji. 'I can work out . . . myself.' He stopped. He was thinking, while peering most intently through his General Tojo spectacles into the black middle distance. Behind us stalls were being dismantled and packed away. 'Leg,' said Bunji. He slightly lifted one leg. 'Over.' He brought it across his other leg, planting it as firmly as he could. He stood there for a moment, forming beneath his waist a bizarre X. Neither of the girls giggled. 'An interesting expression,' he observed eventually.

And then suddenly, without forewarning, he thrust hard at Meadowlark with his cane. '*Rude*,' he charged.

Meadowlark gawped for a moment down at the un-wavering tip. There was a pause while he collected himself. He swallowed twice.

'Is this shrimp threatening me?'

'Yes,' said Bunji. 'I am.' Then he added, to me, 'What is a shrimp?'

'It's like a prawn,' I said. 'Only smaller.'

Meadowlark hesitated. One flat hand moved to push away the accusatory tip, but then he thought better of it.

'This is ridiculous.' He was looking at me. 'Tell him to stop.'

I said nothing.

'Tell him to stop.'

'Cross your fingers and say *pax*.'

'What?'

'Weren't you ever a schoolboy?'

'Eh?' said Bunji, also not understanding.

'He's very sorry,' I said on Meadowlark's behalf.

'Good,' said Bunji. 'The fellow should be.' The tip remained poised for the kill. 'He needs thrashing.' I was impressed by his assured pronunciation.

'He really is very sorry.' The cane was lowered. 'And he's bigger than you,' I added.

Bunji leaned on his stick. Relaxing. Point made.

Yumie and the *yakuza*'s daughter waited quietly.

'You should be careful,' I said to Meadowlark. 'She may

be a mouse but her father's a big cheese in the Wagamama-gumi. It's no laughing matter.'

Meadowlark gazed at me. It was too dark to tell if he was flushed.

'I'm serious,' I said.

'Do they really exist? These . . . Godfathers?'

'Oh they exist,' I said.

'Well they should stamp them out,' said Meadowlark. 'They should do something about her father.'

'I agree. Write to your local Diet Member. Now it's probably better if you say goodbye.'

Meadowlark looked at his watch.

'I really think you should.'

'Well. If you say so.' Again he checked his watch. 'No fun to be had here anyway.'

'No.'

He turned to the others.

'Goodbye,' he said to Yumie and Midori.

They looked at their feet and said nothing.

'Goodbye,' said Bunji grimly, the cane now resting in his palm.

And Meadowlark, somewhat heavily, departed. We watched him trudging alone across the now emptying, unlit field.

At Yumie's request, we walked back towards the massed lights around the station, looking for somewhere to sit down among the competing outlets at street level and stacked above our heads, the buildings striped with illuminated signs all vying for attention. From that bright array she chose a café-restaurant – a huge, sparkling space of obesely upholstered banquettes and seats with swollen backs. There was dark imitation wood throughout the interior complete with bulging cornices and bright copies of Impressionist works on all the walls. Bunji shook his head in serious disapproval, but Yumie tugged at his arm and so we filed in. Immediately ahead of us were some of Monet's water-lilies, painted, I knew, during the battle of Verdun; they floated in luminous stillness behind the hostess's back. To my left, above another table, Manet's harassed beer waitress edged with laden tray past her pipe-smoking customer in his (non-designer) smock. The hostess led us on through busy tables to the more strident pulse of the fenced in open-air area, facing the opalescent street. We passed two Pissarros (I would've liked to stop and look) and then Monet's grain-stacks, gold-lit and blue-shadowed in the early morning near Giverny. The waitresses hurrying around us, lithe and monochrome, were dressed as French chambermaids.

'This is terrible,' Bunji muttered in English as we took our seats.

But Yumie, in Japanese, told him to smile. The restaurant, she continued emphatically, was nice. I watched her enjoy her struggle with the floppy, four-panelled menu. It was late and she was excited.

A waitress came over. Yumie, after cocking her head, a forefinger pressed to her chin as she deliberated, enthusiastically selected ice-cream sundae no. 3 (veined and capillaried with strawberry sauce in the menu photograph) with extra Chantilly cream – her eyes were shining – and a butterscotch milkshake. Midori chose mandarin cheesecake and a chocolate milkshake. I made it two cheesecakes. Bunji cast a last contemptuous glance at the menu, then ordered a small black coffee. He was taking a stand. Against this terrible, stained tide of plastic wood and reproduction Monets and aerated cream. The waitress hesitated only momentarily, then departed, our order noted in microscopic hieroglyphs on her pad. Bunji, satisfied he'd made his point, crossed his arms and surveyed most knowingly the human crush around us. I don't know what it was he knew.

'You're so boring,' Yumie told him in Japanese.

I now noticed a tatty stack of unwanted *manga* comics on a corner table, probably intended for the diversion of solitary afternoon customers. I thought about going over to select one or two.

'Did you see,' Midori said to me in English, 'they have a copy of Renoir's *Boating Party*? I like so much. Do you like it?'

I nodded.

'I asked my father to take us to Europe. To see paintings. But he doesn't like European painting. Or Europe. He will only go for holiday in Japan, or Okinawa. He's too conservative.'

'What are his hobbies?' I asked, reminding myself that this was the *yakuza* with the allegedly customized penis whom we were talking about.

'He likes drinking and eating. He is goo-may. My mother's hobby is shopping. But my grandfather's is calligraphy and gardening,' she added, as if to save her family's reputation. 'What are your hobbies?'

'I don't have any.'

'No?' She was surprised. 'Mine is reading . . . Have you been to Europe?'

'Yes.'

'In one year I will go alone. I will be eighteen. If my father will let me.'

'I hadn't realized your family were traditional.'

'Why, what did you hear about them?'

'Nothing at all,' I assured her.

'I worry for my father.' Midori spoke softly, confidentially. (I knew the reason – Yumie was looking at us, inquisitive-eyed. In a moment she would sweetly, but greedily, demand an unabridged translation.)

'Why?' I asked, interested. 'Why are you worried about him?'

'He works too hard.'

She was looking away from me, across the dozens of buzzing tables.

'Is he successful at his work?' I asked.

'Yes,' she said. 'He is.'

I paused. For some reason which I couldn't quite fathom this had sounded like a threat. I reassured myself by contemplating Midori's pleasant, bookish face; by reminding myself also of her enthusiasm for Jane Austen. I wondered for Meadowlark's sake whether he had in fact been entirely forgotten.

Our food arrived. The sundae's marbled fantasia with its risen head of cream, milkshakes in frosted steel beakers, two solid raisin-studded wedges of cheesecake each with a syrupy layer of mandarin segments and, finally, Bunji's small, principled coffee were unloaded in turn from the tray by our French chambermaid with Asiatic cheekbones.

Yumie immediately got down to work, eyes dipped, her expression growing serious as her long spoon prospected for surprises in the layered lower depths. I excused myself and went over to the corner table with its tattered stack of *manga*.

I picked up several of the comic books and began to browse. *Man Ga*. Irresponsible Pictures. Back at our table, Bunji was taking cool, intermittent sips of his coffee, maintaining his decorum, ignoring the high glass plastered and striped by the wreckage of the sundae within inches of his elbow. Yumie had paused to dab with a paper napkin her ice-cream-daubed mouth. Meanwhile the *yakuza*'s daughter ate slowly, reducing the stolid cheesecake wedge in geometric stages. I returned to the table with my random selection.

Midori was surprised. She did not approve of *manga*.

'I like irresponsible pictures,' I explained.

But she didn't understand.

The size and thickness of telephone directories, they were a free space, unregulated, where the Japanese imagination could riot unrestrained, the bastard offspring of the classical woodblock print, those exercises in clarity, bold colours and strong lines, an art form traditionally concerned with rendering unavoidable Mount Fuji, tangential rain, hunched travellers in clogs crossing arched wooden bridges (while the wind yanked away their straw hats, sent them spiralling aloft), courtesans in walled gardens contemplating chrysanthemums, resplendently robed or (in under-the-counter, *spring picture* versions) tantalizingly semi-robed, then shamelessly disrobed, finally in all-out polymorphous-perverse action, even (for the true Epicureans amongst the dabbling collectors and connoisseurs) being enthusiastically ravished by Hokusai's many-tentacled octopus, its repulsive mollusc mouth clamped tight just below the mount of Venus. (Thus does the artist's mind – and that of the collector – work, compelled, at each turn, to trump itself.) And out of that had come, two centuries later, these irresponsible pictures, selling by the million, shirking responsibility as zealously as the city's swarming workers embraced it. I turned the pages with a disapproving Midori looking on, aware that I was now in free fall in her quiet estimation, especially as one privileged to speak as a mother tongue the language of Jane Austen. If there was a constant theme to the volumes I'd selected (aimed at young men and teenage boys) it seemed to be the violence. At every turn, violence. Parents slapped children, children bullied their peers. A teenage courtship was consummated in defloration by rape. Little seemed to change as the characters and presumably the readership got older. I followed the adventures of a lonely but loveable buck-toothed salaryman with a penchant for boring holes into women's changing rooms. Having served an apprenticeship as a *chikan*, a molester of women on crowded trains – where the bodies press together with asphyxiating force and the *chikan's* hands can make unattributable raids – he now trekked with his tool kit on a quest for revelation through a humming, chiaroscuro metropolis I assumed to be Tokyo (though it could've been any city anywhere and he, with his round eyes, could as easily have been *gaijin* as *nihonjin*), beadily searching out new changing rooms – swimming pools, high schools, hot spring resorts – whose walls he could submit to his expert invasive techniques. I kept turning pages, waiting for a comeuppance which never arrived. Certainly our hero had his reversals, suffering several irate feminine pummellings along the way, but, rubber-limbed and indefatigable, with the unique persistence of the full-time pervert, he would always bounce back to start again, his victims meanwhile remaining strangely shadowy under the artist's pen.

'Oh,' said Yumie.

I looked up. A giant chicken had appeared in the dark sidestreet to our left. This enormous, broad-shouldered fowl carried a placard on a stick brightly promoting the rival deep-fried attractions of the KRAZEE CHICKEN chain. Two very neat Japanese policemen had trapped it there. The creature's infraction was not immediately clear, but I could see a flushed, Caucasian face beneath the lurid red beak and sightless chicken eyes. Then, quite suddenly, the fowl began to scale the fence. Impressively athletic, it had scrambled over within seconds. The startled officers pressed up against the bars, peering in.

Ignoring the astonished customers around it, the desperado chicken turned back to the policemen. It waved a gloved fist. 'You cunts! Yir well ootay fuckin order! Thir's nae need! Nae need! Ootay fuckin order!' The chicken turned away. For a moment it stared suspiciously at the nearby tables of scented, lipsticked teenage girls with their marbled ice-creams and long spoons and luxury milkshakes and dainty designer handbags who were gazing open-mouthed at its yellow feathers and curving beak. 'Stoap starin you cunts!' stormed the chicken, affronted by the anthropological edge to their interest in him. 'Or ah'll gie ye a real fright, ken?' This induced an outbreak of nervous giggling. But, as if now provoked by their preposterous sundaes and their shining identical hair, the quality of their cute little outfits and the lipstick on their childish mouths – as if, despite the proximity of the policemen, it was time to settle scores – the fowl began gesticulating fiercely in response. 'Stoap starin you cunts! Yir all ootay fuckin order! OOTAY FUCKIN ORDER!' The disturbed giggling from the paralysed girls, now like the intense trilling of countless little bells and wind-chimes in a high breeze, reached a crescendo. 'ALL AH YE! OOTAY FUCKIN ORDER!' The creature was turning as it shouted to include us all in its act of remonstration. But then the two very neat policemen jumped it.

The chicken, a storm blown out, restrained by handcuffs, was led away through the tables. The tall fowl went quietly. Its myriad feathers brushed my back and, briefly, I had a strong sense of the human body – sweaty and stubborn and strong – inside that costume. Then they were gone.

'Looks like a marketing disaster for KRAZEE CHICKEN,' I told Bunji.

He nodded sagely. Yumie, smiling nervously, was still gazing after them. Midori, I noticed, was unmoved. But then she was, after all, used to hearing full and frank exchanges of views between *yakuza*. 'Still,' said Bunji, 'it brought back pleasant memories of the Highlands.' He finished his coffee. 'His employers will have to find someone with a work permit next time.'

I heard shouting from across the street. It was the chicken, having rediscovered its voice. It was being manoeuvred, head-first, into the back of a police car. An officer on the pavement now held the confiscated placard, innocently promoting the delights of KRAZEE CHICKEN.

# 10

## THE MEETING

One cold but sunny Wednesday afternoon in December, having decided to take a day's holiday, I was strolling along Omotesando Avenue with no particular purpose in mind when I saw, not far ahead of me, a slowly moving couple. It was Sachiko and an old man, his body perilously bent. Dressed in polyester trousers with a check golfing pattern and a long grey raincoat, he appeared entirely dependent for his balance on her small frame (he wasn't much bigger), his fragile arm thrust through hers, their hands clasping each other, his legs uncertain, balding head dipped, as if pressed down by some unspecified sadness. I came up close behind them. The nape of his neck was quilted by deep lines. Sachiko, hair bound up, was in taut, pale jeans, a short russet jacket and red runners with two-inch soles, white platforms which hardly seemed equal to the task that her slender body had undertaken of carefully supporting this old, unsteady man. She bore an expression of extreme concentration. I realized she was afraid that at any moment he might fall.

'Hullo,' I said in Japanese.

They stopped and gazed at me. The man's eyes were watery, crimson-edged, nesting in wrinkled skin.

'Why you here?' said Sachiko, in English, her tone impatient. Clearly I was not a welcome sight.

'Just walking,' I said.

'This is my grandfather. Grandpa' – reverting now to Japanese – 'this person is from England.'

Her grandfather mumbled something, and then a tremor passed through him. I wondered if he was trying to bow.

'He want say hullo.'

'Where are you going?'

'I take him to doctor. Specialist. Now go home,' said Sachiko. Her grandfather's eyes never left my face. What did he know about his granddaughter? Had he ever surreptitiously felt the fabric of her designer clothes, so petite and so delicate, where they waited for their owner in the wardrobe of her tiny bedroom on long, colourless afternoons passed alone in the cramped family flat one hour and thirty minutes by packed train from Tokyo? How often had he slowly rolled their material between his stubby fingers, and wondered? Whether he had or not, his eyes didn't leave me, as if he'd never seen a foreigner before, a white man with a white face, even though we were often to be seen strolling in this famous, leafy street (of boutiques, of cafés, for the young, not the old like him) and on the TV he watched at home in his room on those long, colourless afternoons.

'I hope you are well, sir,' I said, in Japanese.

'Just old person,' said Sachiko, in English. 'So bad health.'

Another tremor passed the length of his body. She steadied him, with difficulty. It was less her strength than her sheer stubbornness that held him upright on his brittle legs.

'You have a most dutiful granddaughter, sir,' I said, in Japanese.

She smiled, a slight curving of her lips, her nose wrinkling. 'You speak funny. Like long ago. Where you learn?'

'I am a great admirer, sir, of Dazai Osamu,' I told him.

But her grandfather was no longer staring at me, I think because I was looking him right in the eyes as I spoke. He'd lowered his gaze, his clay-coloured lids. He was shy. The top button was missing from his white shirt. I could see the cluster of threads where it should have been.

'Shouldn't you get him a taxi?' I said, in English.

'He needs walk. He sit all day.'

She muttered something in Japanese to him.

They started to walk again along the street. The pavements of Omotesando Avenue are very wide. Pretty girls swinging dainty handbags passed us. Two surly teenage boys with spiky haircuts followed. It was a street for the young with money to spend.

I walked with them.

'I have been learning Japanese for two years, sir. Please excuse my accent.'

'He likes you,' said Sachiko, though her grandfather had not appeared to say anything and was concentrating all his failing powers on maintaining his slow advance, hunching badly, trembling as he did so.

'Keep talking,' she commanded. 'Talk in Japanese. It's funny for him.'

'My great dream, sir, is to travel to the Deep North.' I saw no evidence of his amusement. 'If I ever master the *kanji*, I hope one day to write memorable *haiku*.'

'Funny,' said Sachiko.

'Perhaps *tanka* also.'

We crossed a side road. She said something rapidly in

Japanese. Chiding or perhaps encouraging him. I think he murmured a broken reply.

'He want buy me present,' explained Sachiko. 'Because I am good granddaughter.'

'That's nice.'

We had paused. I gazed at the shop nearest to us. Through the plate glass I could see young faces, thoughtful, strangely solemn, but also glimpses of white teeth as others laughed within its gaudy interior.

'What, from *there*?'

'No,' she said. 'I go alone. Please hold grandpa.'

So I stood there, stupidly holding him, and together we watched his svelte granddaughter, her bottom undeniably shown to best advantage by the splendid workmanship of those taut designer jeans, go confidently into *Condomania*. It is a shop of some renown among those who frequent Omotesando Avenue.

Her grandfather's sunken, crimson-edged eyes blankly contemplated the jazzy façade. I didn't know if the name, spelt out in bright Roman letters, meant anything to him. I wondered if in his youth he had been a frequenter of geisha houses. He trembled, seemed to be slipping. I held him, held him very tight – he was heavier than he looked but at the same time I feared his bones, which I could feel so clearly, sharply through his skin, would snap from the pressure of my grip. We could see Sachiko, at first browsing with a thoughtful expression, then inspecting at close range a display rack beside the window. What had caught her discerning attention? Were they coloured, flavoured, luminous, perhaps decorated with her favourite cartoon characters?

'Truly, it is a wintry day, sir,' I said in Japanese. 'A day to dwell by the fire.'

He turned to stare at me. He looked frightened. 'Sir, does something ail you?' He tried to pull away. 'Sir, you might fall—' But he was pulling, pulling hard, wriggling also, and I was gripping, equally hard, determined not to let go. 'Please, sir. For your granddaughter's sake—'

I could smell him. Smell that cigarettes were an important part of his life. Perhaps that was the problem. Perhaps his body, now so unexpectedly agitated, was crying out for nicotine—

Sachiko came pattering out from the shop on her unnecessarily thick soles.

She began to tell her grandfather off while taking him back, accepting his weight from me. He said nothing. Her arm was threaded through the string handles of a small, skyblue bag of heavy-duty paper. It bore, with a typographical flourish, the legend CONDOMANIA.

Her grandfather, safely transferred, had ceased his struggling. His arms now hung limp and useless. He gazed down vacantly at the clean white pavement of Omotesando Avenue. His slack hands were darkly ridged with veins.

'Silly grandpa,' said Sachiko, I thought quite gently, in Japanese.

We started to walk.

'I'll go,' I said, in English.

'If you want,' she told me, also in English.

'Are you seeing him tonight?' I asked, meaning Meadowlark.

She ignored me, looking fixedly ahead.

'Did you know he carries a torch for you, wherever he goes?'

I knew she couldn't understand that, but she didn't ask me to explain. Just ahead of us was a huge toyshop. The nearest of its broad windows was filled with stuffed furry animals. A woman and her daughter were coming out of the store. The girl, recognizing Sachiko, began to wave and call out animatedly. Sachiko paused. For a moment she looked at them, at the woman, whom her excited friend had started to introduce in the same trilling way. Presumably they had never met before. And then – Sachiko bowed. Bowed deeply.

I had never seen her bow before. The gesture was entirely formal and correct, and accompanied by a respectful greeting for which she lifted her voice to an unusually high pitch, her little arm still threaded through the string handles of the pretty, skyblue bag marked CONDOMANIA. For the first time she had done something which shocked me. Despite her frequently demonstrated mastery of the language, only now, at this moment, did I finally recognize her for what she was: foreign to me, to Meadowlark, *Japanese*, quite beyond the limits of our language, and – though I could easily have reached out and touched her exterior form – utterly remote.

## HOMEWARD BOUND

It's night now. I imagine them on a commuter train, going home. The elevated line passes close to then away from rows of blank windows, the rails intermittently washed, striped by the livid red and green and white of neon lights, tubular or twisted into shapes and ideograms. Sachiko, straphanging, is hemmed in by shoulders and torsos level with her eyes; through the glass she catches occasional glimpses of those familiar lit-up signs, automatically registering them out there in the blackness as there's nothing else to do, her grandfather sitting wedged between silent salarymen, so frail, his head dipped, fitfully sleeping in the carriage's relentless brightness. The windows – seen from below the dark, enormous stanchions – are a luminous yellow strip which runs the length of the disappearing train. Sachiko will not hear the mournful warning clang clang, clang clang at the level crossing ahead of them, foretelling their still invisible approach as the barriers either side simultaneously descend and pedestrians, cyclists, cars pause under streetlamps, waiting for the sudden fierce whoosh of passing carriages, and for a moment (just a moment) see, behind long oblong glass, the commuting bodies, the etiolated faces, before the train – including the swaying Sachiko and her fitfully sleeping grandfather – has gone, is just two dwindling pinpricks of red light, and the barriers can begin to rise.

# 11

## I WOULD HAVE PREFERRED YOU TO THEM

When I went drinking with Bunji, he liked to take me to Tsukuda-jima, a quarter of Tokyo lapped by the Sumida river; this was an old part of the city whose cheerful, somewhat shabby denizens, Tokyo cockneys – their speech rapid, noisy, the accent distinctive – were proud to be *Edokko*, children of Edo (the city's former name), meaning they, their parents and grandparents had not been part of that great population influx of the fifties and sixties but were *chaki chaki*, native to the capital. An older, more truculent Japan was to be found here, in these narrow streets, the drab houses divided from each other by the regular incision of alleyways, grubby-walled, squatting beneath a low-slung net of power lines, washing suspended from eaves and small balconies, the entire glowering district now over-shadowed by concrete waterfront developments, speculative towers of condominiums, atriums, empty investment flats whose soft-lit lifts rose percolated by muzak. With Bunji I would search out dives tucked away among these surly streets, convinced they came closer in spirit to the pre-war bars of Ginza where Dazai Osamu would have frittered away long alcoholic days than his own old haunts' flashy, brass- and leather-trimmed successors.

Meadowlark, however, had no interest in such places. And so we found ourselves, one evening, back in the bar where Harvey and his companion had won the competition for Mamiko and Tomoko months before. It was a Friday. During a long and difficult day of furious telephone calls and faxes, when it had seemed we might be losing our grip on a deal expected to earn impressive fees, Symons, lead partner on the transaction, had shouted at Meadowlark. Had loudly, publicly lamented that my colleague no longer seemed to be the person he once was. Had, while doing so, flung papers on the floor. And had then jerked a freshly minted fax from the hands of a terrified secretary and (most theatrically I thought) ripped it sharply in two.

So now, after all this, Meadowlark wanted to drink. He demanded two bottled beers each and finished the first of his immediately.

'You're falling apart,' I told him.

He started on his second bottle, ignoring me. A young and heavily made-up woman with waist-length hair was seated at the adjoining table. She had cerise lips. Her thickly powdered skin, giving her gaze a stark, preternatural quality, would have been better suited to a geisha than a modern girl; it was as if someone had burst a packet of flour in her face. Meadowlark, tip of the bottle resting against his parted mouth, slyly eyed her. But then she stood, and moved to another table.

'You're losing it,' I said. His Adam's apple oscillated vigorously as he gulped down the urine-coloured liquid. 'The old charm.'

Meadowlark banged down his beer. 'Fuck off,' he softly advised me.

'As someone said today, you're no longer the person you once were.'

He began waving an arm. He wanted another drink.

'How are your parents?'

'What?'

'I said, how are your parents?'

'Why do you want—' he began, swivelling his head and torso, leaning over me, 'to know about my parents?'

His breath, rich with alcohol, fanned my face. I sipped at my own beer. 'Why don't we,' he continued, 'talk about *your* parents?'

The waiter came over.

'*Biru o kudasai*,' Meadowlark demanded, flourishing his bottle. 'Two,' he added as an afterthought, showing two fingers. 'TWO.'

'Is this wise?'

But he only cursed me again.

'You've an enriched vocabulary these days.'

'Good,' said Meadowlark.

'No longer wet behind the ears, eh?'

He was watching the cerise-lipped girl with the baking-powder face where she sat at her new table.

'I hope you don't talk like that in front of Her Majesty.'

Harvey was standing at the bar with two colleagues, neither of whom I recognized. They were drinking champagne. 'Looks like they've had their Christmas bonus.'

A young Caucasian woman with blonde bangs in a dark red matching skirt and jacket joined them. I heard her laughing. Swilling her drink and laughing. Lipsticked mouth apart: HAR HAR HAR HAR HAR. It crossed the room to where Meadowlark and I sat. HAR HAR HAR HAR HAR. She was one of the boys. 'I wish we got a Christmas bonus.'

HAR HAR HAR HAR HAR.

Harvey came over. The woman with blonde bangs followed.

'How was Bangkok?' I asked.

'Not in mixed company,' said Harvey, casually leaning against the wall.

'They shagged their way round Thailand.' HAR HAR HAR HAR HAR. The dark-red-suited woman bellowed most heartily at her own remark. Under the soft, expensive fabrics which enclosed her, she was powerfully built.

'What on earth gave you that idea?' said Harvey amiably.

(Suddenly I saw them. In another bar. Three thousand miles away. T-shirted. Moneyed. Free to trade. There were soft bodies waiting in the scarlet dark. A pimp wearing a fat Swiss wristwatch – the timepiece heavy with gold and that charming Swiss attention to detail – drew up a stool.)

'What on earth gave you that idea?' said Harvey amiably.

'I know everything. Roger told me ... Roger the – rogerer!' she exultantly exclaimed. HAR HAR HAR HAR HAR. 'Roger the rogerer.' Her hand, formed into a fist, shadow-jabbed at Harvey's chest in celebration of this happy coinage.

'She's pissed,' said Harvey.

'Of course I am. Where's the fucking champagne?'

'Did you go to the wedding?'

'Cancelled!' shouted the woman, turning back to us with a flick of those blonde bangs. 'Wise girl. I said where's the fucking champagne?'

'You've already asked that,' said Harvey.

'Did I?'

She set off for the bar. She was wearing black tights. Her short hem-line revealed broad, muscular hams.

'Mariko and Keiko are joining me later,' said Harvey. 'Great bodies.'

'They're all right,' said Meadowlark, unimpressed.

'You know them?' I asked.

'I've seen them around.' He was now on his fourth bottle.

HAR HAR HAR HAR HAR.

Harvey turned to see what was happening at the bar. The woman in the dark red suit brandished a two-thirds full bottle of champagne at him.

'I'll speak to you later,' said Harvey. He headed back to his companions.

'She's being picked up,' muttered Meadowlark mournfully.

'Eh?'

'Over there.' He indicated with a finger.

He meant the girl with the cherry-stained mouth and white, geisha's face. She was slim, small-breasted. Two tall Caucasian men in suits, both in their forties, one balding, had seated themselves at her table. They looked like bank managers. We watched as the girl briefly nodded and smiled. Encouraged, the more hirsute of the two spoke and gestured expansively. She started to giggle. 'He's getting off with her,' said Meadowlark, annoyed.

'How's Sachiko?'

'She's a bitch,' said Meadowlark. He took my half-drunk beer and placed it beside his four empty bottles. Despite his fleshy bulk, Meadowlark's tolerance to alcohol was low and his cheeks were now glazed with a beetroot flush.

'Surely not.'

'I'll prove it to you.' He fumbled for and eventually withdrew his mobile phone from an inside pocket. He dialled a number. 'Here. Listen.'

It was a recorded voice. I recognized it as Sachiko's.

'Why don't you leave a message?'

'What's she doing?' He drank from my commandeered bottle. 'The bitch never tells me what she's doing.'

'Homework?' I suggested.

Meadowlark began shouting for another beer. A startled waiter hurried over. 'Two,' said Meadowlark. 'TWO *kudasai*.' The Japanese waiter's eyes and expression gave no clue to his private thoughts about this swollen, scarlet-cheeked *gaijin*. He acknowledged the order and left.

'I'm seeing her later,' said Meadowlark in a quieter voice.

'So where's the problem?'

'She's bringing her grandfather.'

'On a Friday night?'

'It's meant to be a secret. She's supposed to be at home babysitting him.'

'Is she taking him to Kabukicho?'

'No. To play pachinko.'

'Harvey's signalling us.'

'It's his dying wish, apparently,' said Meadowlark.

'Harvey's still waving.'

'Who cares?' His tone now was more maudlin than aggressive. One vast hand was pressed to the side of his head, cupping and supporting it, elbow on the table. Harvey turned his back on us. The waiter came up, dropped off two bottles, then hurried away. I realized he was frightened of Meadowlark.

My companion, with a great slurred grunt, straightened himself and hoisted up the nearest of the new consignment.

He drank while he watched, beadily, the girl with the light-cherry mouth and baking-powder face being courted by the older white men. The bald one was nodding hopefully to the music. There was something faintly cadaverous about him. I thought he thought his friend was in with a better chance. Each would have, I knew, a wife, and maybe a child, in a glittering three-bedroom flat (annual rent 6,000,000 yen a year, paid for by his employer) within a one-mile radius of their circular chrome-rimmed table. The girl with cerise lips would know this also.

'Don't you think she's overdone the make-up?' I asked.

Meadowlark slowly turned to look at me. 'Sometimes, you know,' he eventually said, 'I can't stand you.'

'It's okay, I know you're drunk.'

'I'd say it if I was sober.'

'I wonder which of those men has the bigger flat.'

Meadowlark put down his bottle. It was empty. His hand moved unsteadily to the next one and throttled its neck.

The two gentlemen with large, well-appointed flats were standing up. Cerise lips did not. They stood there, looking down at her. The bald one was silent. His companion did the talking. Revealing a slight smile, she gently shook her head.

With a glassy crack, one of Meadowlark's collection of bottles fell. I instinctively jerked round. It rolled its way to the edge of our table, but then stopped.

'Did you know . . .' he began.

'Did I know what?'

His face, I thought, was sad. He was no longer drinking, although his great hand remained closed around the final unfinished bottle. Alcohol furred his words. '. . . what she sells.'

'Who?'

'Sachiko.' He'd slumped back once again in his seat, his arms resting heavy and inert on the tabletop. 'She sells her knickers . . . did you know that?' He didn't move. Didn't try to straighten himself. 'Yes. She even sells her used knickers . . . Two thousand yen a throw . . . This . . . shop buys them. Have to be used . . . of course.'

'Of course.'

'*Soiled*. No use if they're clean.'

'No.'

'Schoolgirl's. Have to be a schoolgirl's.'

'Sure,' I said. 'Have to.'

'With a photo. Showing the proud owner. That she's really still at school . . . Like a hallmark.'

'Sure,' I said. 'Have to.'

'And men, old men, salarymen, buy them . . . from this . . . shop . . . Each one with a matching photo . . . There's even a dispenser . . . an automatic dispenser . . . for the shy ones.'

Meadowlark paused.

I waited.

'Want to buy one?'

'No thank you,' I said.

'Get you a discount.'

'For old times' sake?'

'Exactly.' He paused. Ground the glass base of his bottle against the tabletop. 'She laughs at them.'

'At who?'

'Her . . . customers.' He continued grinding against the table's surface. 'She's only sixteen.'

'I know.'

'And she thinks men are ridiculous.'

'All men?'

'She thinks we're ridiculous.' Meadowlark lifted up his beer, peered into its dark glass for a moment, then thought better of it and returned the bottle to the table. 'She despises us.'

120

'Surely not.'

'Oh she does,' insisted Meadowlark, almost, it seemed, with a certain perverse contentment at this thought. 'She does.'

He paused again; then scratched thoughtfully at his nose.

'Do you think we are?' he suddenly asked me, his bull's neck twisting. He stank of beer. 'I'm sick of thinking about her, you know. Sick of thinking about her body. I don't want to think about it anymore.'

'I see,' I said.

'No you don't. Of course you don't . . . You're a cold fish. How could you?'

We were both silent after that. The bar was filling up. I could no longer hear Harvey and his companions. The girl with cerise lips was blocked off by intervening bodies. The lights had been dimmed and the music turned up. There was a loudspeaker immediately above our heads and the multi-layered electronic noise pounded down against our unprotected skulls.

'When are you meeting her?'

Meadowlark didn't answer. In a gloomy, distracted way he palpitated his flushed neck.

'Are we?' he finally said.

'I'm sorry?'

'Ridiculous . . . Do you know what I do at work? When I think of her . . . of what she . . . does . . . Because she isn't there . . . Do you know what I have to do? . . . So I can carry on . . . Why—' he tried to straighten himself, but without success, trembling the table and its precarious glass load, trapped in the centre of a stale alcoholic fug, 'why do we have to work? That's what I ask myself now. Why do we have to work? . . . I tell you. *She's bleeding me dry.*'

He paused once more, glassy eyes gazing straight ahead. 'You know,' he eventually continued, in a more subdued voice, 'I saw my first *chikan* on the underground yesterday. He was operating the Yamanote line. It wasn't that busy. He was taking a chance. I spotted him and then he . . . saw me. God, he looked surprised.' Meadowlark snorted. 'Don't think he'd ever been spotted by a white man before. I tell you, he was an ugly little shit.'

'Did they catch him?'

'The girls are too ashamed to say anything, aren't they?'

'Usually,' I said.

And then Meadowlark, without warning, stood. The table shuddered and all his carefully assembled bottles fell. Briefly he stared down at the wreckage. Then he began, one by one, to right them. I had no idea why.


## ONE SCENE FROM THE PACHINKO PARLOUR

It's the noise which strikes you first. Constant. Unvarying. It demands the mind's submission.

*hrrrsh! shinnng! hrrrsh! shinnng!*

The high-ceilinged interior is silvery, full of reflections. Row after row of pachinko machines.

Solitary men and women, romantic couples, husbands and wives sat side by side down all the luminous chrome steel aisles, absorbed as they steadily fed in ball-bearings, long gleaming queues of them click click clicking their way through each machine's single aperture – the players watching, expressionless, cataleptic, as the tiny steel balls ricocheted wildly behind the glass, briefly living out in those surreal interiors irrational, chaotic lives.

*hrrrsh! shinnng! hrrrsh! shinnng!*

I'd read of a couple whose toddler daughter had been left to wander the aisles while they played. And while they played, entranced, a man had seized her and taken her away and done things to her body.

*hrrrsh! shinnng! hrrrsh! shinnng!*

Sachiko pressed coins into a slot to purchase ball-bearings for her grandfather. They rattled down. He sat there, gazing with an air of stupefaction into the interior of his pachinko machine with its waiting wheels and mazy whorls of pinhead tracks, while his granddaughter (wearing a Calvin Klein leather jacket, her hair down, glossy, loose, looking older than her sixteen years) bent over to lift and firmly guide his leathery hand to the handle which controlled the aperture.

In the next seat along sat a plain woman in her late thirties, bespectacled, hair twisted to a tight bun, an endless steel army marching into (and gushing, clattering out of) her machine. With cool expertise, while drawing on a cigarette, she paused to tip her latest winnings into a plastic box already heaped with ball-bearings.

His neighbour's prowess appeared to intimidate Sachiko's grandfather (I caught him looking at her from the corner of his crimson-edged eye). He seemed to hesitate. But Sachiko turned his hand—

*hrrrsh! shinnng! hrrrsh! shinnng!*

As the balls spat frantically about behind the glass in their mad pinball world, a strange smile spread across his face. Above him, her milky hand still upon his, Sachiko leaned closer, fascinated, concentrating. With her hair unbound, so thick, so rich, I could not deny, that day, she was beautiful. I felt a spark of jealousy, jealousy of Meadowlark, glow somewhere inside me.

And behind us the subject of that jealousy complained suddenly, loudly, his voice still clumsy from alcohol, 'Did you see how he looked at me?' He didn't seem to care that Sachiko might hear. 'What right has *he* got to look at *me* like that? When I think of what he probably did in the war.'

Sachiko and her grandfather were enjoying success. Two or three ball-bearings stuttered out and then a whole rush of them. They were starting to accumulate. The old man's odd, thin smile remained and his watery eyes glowed. He allowed his granddaughter to guide his shrivelled hand.

'Don't you agree?' persisted Meadowlark.

'What?'

'I said don't you agree. What right has he got to look at me like that?'

'I didn't notice anything.'

'Of course you did,' he insisted. 'That look he gave me . . . Well, I'll give him a look. If he's not careful . . . War criminal.'

They were losing now. Their stash was diminishing. Sachiko put in more coins. Her grandfather's hand, suddenly uncovered, was trembling furiously.

*hrrrsh! shinnng! hrrrsh! shinnng!*

'Where can you get a beer round here?' demanded Meadowlark. He wandered off, somewhat unsteadily, down the aisle. Attendants, bemused by this inexplicable apparition, a hulking, listing *gaijin*, parted to let him through. If I was jealous of him, then he was jealous of Sachiko's grandfather. I saw how gently she covered and held his jactitating hand. And perhaps, while they played, he remembered a time when she'd been tiny enough for him to hold her, all of her, wriggling with life between his hands, balanced on a knee. I looked from him to his granddaughter. Her leather jacket must have cost five hundred pounds. I glanced behind me. Meadowlark had disappeared. I had never found out (and never would) what it was she did to satisfy him.

*hrrrsh! shinnng! hrrrsh! shinnng!*

Meadowlark returned. He must have gone outside to the vending machines. An open litre-sized bottle of Suntory beer bulged in his hand.

'Are you sure about that?' I said.

Meadowlark crowded in beside me to get a better view, lifting the bottle to his mouth as he did so. Sachiko and her grandfather had started winning again. A platoon of ball-bearings rattled out. She was leaning forward, chattering into the old man's ear.

'Want?' Cold glass was being pressed into my face.

'Maybe later,' I said.

'Can't hold it, can you?'

'No,' I conceded.

*hrrrsh! shinnng! hrrrsh! shinnng!*
*hrrrsh! shinnng! hrrrsh! shinnng!*

'I think the expression,' I said, 'is superfluous to requirements.'

Meadowlark placed a hand on Sachiko's shoulder. Without turning, she shrugged it off. Ball-bearings cascaded. Their receptacle was brimming.

'War criminal,' muttered Meadowlark and drifted away again with his beer. The attendants, I saw, had their eyes on him. He paused behind a stiff-backed, middle-aged couple, drinking and watching them as they played their machines. They became aware of him. Twice the man glanced over his shoulder. Meadowlark winked at him and brought the bottle to his lips. The man spoke to his wife. They were uncomfortable. Their game began to suffer. Without a word they stood, in unison, and quietly headed up the aisle to two vacant places at the very end.

Meadowlark raised his bottle in silent, unsteady acknowledgement of their departure.

Behind me, Sachiko screamed.

Her grandfather had slumped forward, his glabrous head hanging limply, like an old marionette whose strings have been cut, and she was trying, struggling furiously, hands forced beneath his arms, to lift him.

I ran down the aisle shouting the Japanese word for water.

*hrrrsh! shinnng! hrrrsh! shinnng!*

He was carried out on a human chair, formed by two attendants who'd crossed arms and linked hands. His head lolled as they hurried down the aisle to the fresh air, the water he'd been unable to properly drink seeping from the corners of his mouth.

Outside they set him down on a bench. Sachiko was

frightened. She'd already declined the manager's offer of an ambulance. All she wanted was a taxi to take them home.

'You should take him to a hospital,' I said in Japanese.

'No, *home*,' she insisted, in petulant English. I knew why. In two hours her parents and brother would return from her aunt's in Kamakura. Under the Calvin Klein leather jacket there was still just a child.

Meadowlark, meanwhile, hovered ineffectually behind the two waiting attendants. Earlier he'd tried to offer his bottle of beer to her inert grandfather. I'd had to dissuade him. The manager of the pachinko parlour, a short Korean in a dark suit, had come out. He squatted on his haunches beside Sachiko's grandfather, whose head hung down, motionless, and felt the old man's temples.

'Why won't you get us a taxi?' Sachiko complained to him in Japanese.

But the Korean again proposed an ambulance.

'I want go home!' Sachiko screamed in English – at me and at Meadowlark, who'd now pushed his way forward between the attendants, dwarfing them. She'd begun to cry. Her thin eyes glittered with tears.

Then she swung back to her grandfather where he sat, unmoving and uncomprehending, now leaning to one side. Her little milk-white hand beat like a wing, desperately trying to fan his face. The Korean, still on his haunches, fingers holding the old man's wrist, said something which caused her to flare again. She still wanted her taxi. She was going to have her taxi. 'Help grandpa!' she snapped at Meadowlark. Then she saw the cab.

She ran to the kerb, flapping her hands, shouting hysterically. The low white car glided to a halt. Its passenger door swung slowly open. She continued her clamour, leaning into the unlit interior. Finally a light came on, and then the driver cautiously emerged.

He blinked, bewildered, as he slowly took in the tight cluster of people watching him from around the bench. He wore a drab blue suit, thin grey tie and white gloves.

'Look at his gloves,' said Meadowlark, slurring his words. 'I hate those gloves.'

The taxi-driver, though Sachiko urged him on, took his time, almost ambling from his car to where we stood while she fretted around him, keeping up her unrelenting soprano clamour. Eventually he reached us, pausing in front of the inert figure of her grandfather. I could see that he was reluctant to become involved.

A three-way disputation now began. The driver was laconic, almost monosyllabic. He was a youngish man with an odd, triangular port-wine stain on his neck. The Korean continued to press the case for an ambulance. Sachiko complained and threatened and demanded in her quavering voice. She wanted the taxi-driver to join her in manoeuvring her grandfather to his car. But he remained reluctant. He looked to the Korean for a lead.

Then Meadowlark stepped in among them.

'Carry grandpa!' Sachiko shrilled at him. 'Carry grandpa!'

And Meadowlark – without a word – did. With one great hoarse grunt he hoisted him up, limp and loose-limbed as a doll in his arms. And then he was heading away from us, towards the taxi.

It took the driver a moment to understand what was happening. When he suddenly did, he yelled, then dashed after Meadowlark and his human load.

Beside the waiting vehicle an argument began. The driver didn't want a sick body in his car. The body, in Meadowlark's vast arms, appeared to move, as if to remind the driver it was still alive. But the driver was adamant. He did not want a sick body propped up, drooling helplessly, inside the pristine white interior of his car.

But finally Meadowlark appeared to tire of this debate, of his drink-dislocated English bouncing pointlessly against the equally impenetrable surface of the driver's dogged Japanese. He dipped down and bundled the barely moving body onto the back seat. There it slumped, sprawled on the stretched white nylon covering so eerie to the touch.

The driver shouted. He tried to reach into his taxi. But Meadowlark kept between him and the door. The driver continued to shout. He did not want to become involved. He was worried about his vehicle.

At this Sachiko came running forward, hurling high-pitched instructions. She was telling the driver her address, making him aware that she lived one hour and thirty minutes by packed train from the centre of Tokyo.

And, for the first time, he must have thought about the potential size of his fare, for he stopped shouting and now began, his eyes highly suspicious, to gauge the little girl in the leather jacket with the long rich hair which maybe, in happier circumstances, he would have daydreamed of running his hands through, trying to decide if she was likely to have the cash for a journey deep into Tokyo's hinterland of satellite towns.

Behind me the Korean said softly (in Japanese) to his attendants, 'Call an ambulance.' One of them left.

'Give him money,' Sachiko was telling Meadowlark, as if she'd overheard that quiet command. '*Give him money.*'

But the taxi-driver had now reached a decision. And,

while Meadowlark was searching for money, he tried again to reach inside his car.

I don't know what he intended to do, but he was halfway in, obscuring the slack figure of Sachiko's grandfather, who sat there, unable to move, like a rich man waiting for his chauffeur, when Meadowlark, dropping his wallet, tackled the driver.

They scuffled. Meadowlark was shouting. He was shouting, 'Take off those fucking gloves!' and, without waiting for a response, was attempting to remove them himself.

'Why is he taking his gloves off?' one of the attendants asked the manager.

'English custom,' said another attendant. 'Don't fight with your gloves on.'

'Go home,' Sachiko was shrieking as the two men grappled. 'We want go home!'

Meadowlark was holding the driver's wrist. Was exerting tremendous force on that single spot. The driver, even as he struggled, was staring in amazement as one white glove, now almost completely unpeeled, was yanked from his fingers, revealing his hand. But Meadowlark wasn't finished. He was pulling now at the other glove, the cotton fabric stretching until it too began to reluctantly unpeel, then was suddenly gone, had come away in the Englishman's fingers, exposing the other, equally ordinary, hand. The driver broke free from Meadowlark's grip, retreating to bend double, palms on knees, wheezing hoarsely. The two crumpled gloves lay forgotten on the pavement.

Meadowlark, also winded, backed away. What he had done was beginning to sink in, I could see that on his face. Behind him the night-time square was filling with people. A giant screen high on the side of one of the tallest buildings flickered with vast colour images. When I glanced up they were promoting a yoghurt. Excited children, each face momentarily larger than a house, lapped up this delicious new achievement wielding enormous gleaming spoons. Then we saw the yoghurt pot's surface, wide as a swimming pool as it was stirred, opening up a great, lush, creamy spiral.

Sachiko's mobile phone began to ring. She struggled to pull it from her bag and then shrieked into its glow. Her lipstick was smeared to her cheeks, her mascara had run. Her voice began, almost despite herself, an argument with the caller. I realized it was her father. She swung away, into the shadows. I could still hear her voice but none of the words. An ambulance was drawing up, immediately behind the taxi. When she saw it, she screamed with renewed force into the mobile then flung it to the ground. It bounced once and lay there while she rushed back towards the taxi. Her grandfather still sat there in darkness and regal silence, like a king asleep.

Those previously clustered around the bench now moved towards the kerb. Two ambulancemen had appeared, were leaning into the taxi while a third restrained a struggling Sachiko. She didn't want them to touch him. That much I could make out. I followed the others to the kerbside, passing her discarded mobile. I bent and picked it up. I lifted it to my face. A Japanese man was shouting. His muffled voice filled my ear. I moved the phone away a fraction. Then another. His voice now seemed smaller, fainter, the angry voice of a man one hour and thirty minutes by packed train from the centre of Tokyo, a train he had travelled on for twenty years and would have to travel on for another twenty, whether he wanted to or not. I don't know why he kept on shouting but he did, ignorant of who his daughter really was, or perhaps half-suspecting, but powerless, ignorant also of Meadowlark, who'd now come up close to me, silent and shamefaced, head bowed. I moved the phone away another inch; I could no longer hear him, Sachiko's father, but I didn't doubt he was still yelling. Meadowlark's broad hand closed unexpectedly around mine, taking the phone from me. I couldn't resist the greater power of his grip. He brought it close to his own face.

'Hello,' he said. '*Konban wa.*' I waited. I could imagine the surprise at the other end of that line. 'I'm sorry,' said Meadowlark. 'I'm sorry about your father.' I heard the ambulance doors close. I looked across. The taxi was now empty. I couldn't see Sachiko. 'I'm sorry,' repeated Meadowlark quietly. Then he switched off the phone.


## BEHIND GLASS

I watch him through my glass partition and his. It is clear he can't (or doesn't want to) concentrate on his work, despite the piles beginning to heap up on his desk. I can see the files awaiting his due diligent attention, and he is trying, but failing, to give them that attention, bending over sheaves of paper loosely joined on a treasury tag, in white shirt and braces, sleeves rolled up. I can see he is making no progress. Rubbing his broad face. He is tired of it all, of all the paper – he who once embraced paper. It is as if he might explode, suddenly explode, spattering frustrated scraps of flesh against the glass partition which walls him in.

# PART TWO

# 12

## THE IMPORTANCE OF CLIENT CARE

Visible through the firmly closed door of no. 2 meeting room (suitable for six persons or less) were Meadowlark's left shoulder-blade, our partner Harry Vickers's back and head, and Sanderson, his narrow face white as candlewax. I didn't have to hear to know that the client was registering a very long and convoluted complaint. (I'd heard him in action, I knew how he liked to talk, building his sentences slowly, subclause by subclause, into strange labyrinthine structures better suited to a *roman fleuve* than to doing business.) Nor did I have to hear to know that this complaint concerned the owner of the large left shoulder-blade. That, at least, remained stiffly alert, unmoved, though I couldn't see how the rest of his body was reacting to the waxen face's onslaught, for this was what – as I passed and then, discreetly, repassed – it seemed to become, Sanderson having stoked himself up from relatively subtle beginnings. Vickers was trying, but without success, to play the placatory role. (I knew he would *deal* with Meadowlark later.) I returned to my room.

Sitting down, I dictated two letters, keeping it snappy, winding back in squeaky snatches to edit them down even further, make them even snappier, wondering if it was possible to write a legal letter in the style of Dazai Osamu, speculating what he could have made of them (while off his face on drink and drugs); then, deciding that shaving off any more words might leave them rather too gnomic if not ironic (our clients didn't pay for irony), I moved on, leaving these finger-flexing exercises for the grandiloquent pre-cedent which I now opened on my screen. Referring to it, I dictated half a contract for the swollen file which had squatted on my desk for two weeks now like a fat, ugly reproach, the cardboard wallet overstuffed and splitting. I had paused to check a point of fact, was pulling out wads of the papery stuffing in search of it, when I heard an unexpected shout, followed moments later by two shorter, equally surprised shouts. I looked up.

Meadowlark was no longer in no. 2 meeting room. He was standing with his back to my glass partition. Curiously, he seemed both broader and taller than when I'd last seen him, just half an hour before. I opened my door. He turned his head. I could see he was sweating. There was an unusual light in his eyes, which had widened also, as if some remarkable event had just occurred.

'What's up?'

He stared at me most keenly, as if I too had changed. 'I've just hit Sanderson,' he explained.

'That's the second person this month.'

Meadowlark rubbed at his crown with the heel of one palm.

'What's going on?' I said.

'Eh?'

'I said what's going on?' I stepped out of my room. 'Second person this month.'

Meadowlark merely rubbed again at his crown, slowly

rotating his palm, keeping his dreamy gaze on me. He had about him an air of obtusity, as if it were he who'd taken the blow, and that slow dull rubbing was meant to dispel the resulting fog. 'Head's killing me,' he observed, unnecessarily. 'Been like this all morning.' He now began to manoeuvre out of his jacket while pulling at his constricting tie. He let the jacket sprawl at his feet, and then proffered his bulging hand. It took a moment to realize he was offering me his tie. It was dark blue with green spots. 'Take it,' said Meadowlark portentously, as if he were offering me his birthright.

'Are you sure?'

'Take it.'

So I took it. Rejection might have been misinterpreted. There could have been the ignominy of being garrotted – right there – with a dark blue tie covered in green spots. Briefly his hand touched mine as that balled-up length of silk passed between us. His skin was slippery and hot.

'Keep it,' said Meadowlark.

'I don't know what to say.'

'I won't be needing it again. I've got forty-seven. Can have them all if you like.' He paused, toed his vast splayed jacket. 'Can have this also . . .'

He had no chance to offer me anything else as Vickers now appeared at the end of the corridor – with Sanderson. Sanderson was pressing a tissue to his nose, the scrunched-up ball tinctured red. Vickers, arms angrily swinging, came towards us. He stopped beside my glass partition.

'I think you'd better go back to your room for the moment,' he advised Meadowlark, his face oddly striated, 'while I see Mr Sanderson out.'

'Come on.' I tried to lead Meadowlark away. It was like

tugging at a vast iron structure. Nothing at all moved.

'I really would suggest you go to your room,' Vickers persisted grimly.

Then, suddenly, Meadowlark was moving down the corridor, moving with purpose towards Sanderson. Vickers made an ineffectual grab at his arm but Meadowlark, who dwarfed him, passed without noticing.

'Stop him.' Vickers was panicking. *'Stop him for Chrissake.'*

Meadowlark was now level with Sanderson. The client (knowing his interminable sentences offered no protection) backed hastily against a door. I caught up with them.

Meadowlark paused to rub again at his skull. 'Bloody ache's killing me.'

'Aspirin?' I proposed.

He thought about this, then shook his head.

'No. I'm going outside.' He paused to scrape again at his troublesome skull. 'This is bloody killing me.' And with that he was gone.

## RAIN

He leaves. Not bothering with his raincoat or umbrella, abandoning both despite the rain, the sad constant Tokyo rain, morosely hunching his great shoulders, walking quickly, ignoring passers-by whom he knocks as he passes – they turn to stare and mutter after this rude and intimidating *gaijin* who is not only walking without looking but is, in fact, zigzagging, the lengths irregular, the angles too. It's clear this monster, this big-nosed devil (for these Westerners do indeed have such large, bizarre noses, they blare like trumpets when blown, so coarse, why do they require them to be that size? – a thought which had occurred to me also the first time I'd returned to London after six months in Japan, sitting on the tube going home from Heathrow to Wimbledon, looking about the dirty carriage, marvelling at the extraordinary size of all the noses, the sheer mess and confusion of those Caucasian faces, suddenly missing intensely the dark-haired harmony of Tokyo), yes, clear this foreigner is not quite right as he haphazardly zigzags, ignoring totally the world around him, resiling from his duty, his social obligation, to look out for his neighbour (since he keeps on barging them), ignoring the police (though those he occasionally passes, wearing transparent plastic stretched like cellophane wrapping over their smart white-peaked caps to protect them from the rain, are certainly not ignoring him, they know how every so often – it happens, it's unfortunate – a *gaijin* will lose it, go out of control, just like a rogue elephant, maddened, stampeding for no good reason); no longer hunching, indeed lifting his face to receive the cooling benediction of the rain, on he goes, ignoring the wide glass frontage of Marui Department Store, ignoring a brief, neat file of Korean schoolgirls in traditional dress, when he could have paused instead to consider the ambiguous status of Japan's largest minority, ignoring also the large parked van atop of which stands a white-bearded man in dark suit and tie broadcasting pro-Emperor, revanchist propaganda over twin loudspeakers (which no one listens to and Meadowlark can't anyway understand and, besides, that sagaciously bearded patriot has no interest in or designs upon Meadowlark's irrelevant *gaijin* soul which is welcome to stew in liberal filth and corruption if it so chooses). The rain is coming down fiercer and fiercer now. Shoppers as they enter the supermarket which he nears pause thoughtfully to manoeuvre their furled, dripping umbrellas into transparent plastic sheaths, thin and disposable, tugged from a dispenser, but Meadowlark ignores the supermarket, the counters of food which stretch out of sight, the extraordinary culinary plenitude, the bundled sticks of meat, the raw fish, the imported whisky, the melon which costs twelve pounds, on he continues, still zigzagging, ignoring also the sushi bars, the yakitori joints, the pizza parlours, the traditional Japanese tea-shops, the ersatz-French cafés, the *ramen-ya*, the *robatayaki*, the Brazilian/Israeli/Ethiopian curiosities, the beer gardens (where unbuxom waitresses masquerade hopefully as buxom Bavarian bar maids), the £300 a head *kaiseki* establishments, the blow-fish restaurants (all poison sacs removed, a government licence on the wall), all crowding in, jostling for right of access to Meadowlark's stomach and Meadowlark's wallet, yet on he goes, past a mortgage broker – which he also ignores, but then he has no interest in signing up for a multi-generation mortgage so he too can buy a family home within the dense sprawl of Tokyo – still zigzagging, face still upturned, receiving the rain, letting it splash off his chilled skin, ignoring everything, the inside of his head a bloody, cymbal-clashing riot—

Or so I imagined it. In any event, by the next day he had disappeared.

# 13

**THE DISAPPEARANCE**

I telephoned him several times that night, but there was no answer. Just his machine. Deciding it was best to let him wind himself down, I gave up after the fourth call and waited to see if he made it to the office the next day. He didn't. I then rang directory enquiries in England and obtained his parents' number, but couldn't bring myself to call them. It was unlikely, anyway, that they would know anything. Instead I spent a difficult hour with Harry Vickers which he twice interrupted to put in his own call to Meadowlark. This time the phone rang without even the answering machine clicking into action. I said I had no idea what had been happening to him. Vickers nodded, but he looked unconvinced when I told him I rarely saw Meadowlark outside the office. That he had mentioned nothing to me.

'I can't understand it.' Vickers was a man of about fifty-five, with meagre sandy hair and a permanently crumpled expression. Though he moved decisively about the office and steadily churned out tapes in his Mancunian accent, clasping his dictaphone like a man of action, he had always struck me as having the air of someone deeply tired, as if that decisiveness, that productivity, was all a continually willed thing which, if he ever released his grip, would simply evaporate to nothing. 'I always thought he was a bit stiff when he joined, but I never expected . . . I mean, I thought it would be better for everyone if he loosened up, lost some of that reserve. I suppose it's his size, makes him shy, but . . .' The tired face gave a tired smile. 'It's one thing to loosen up, another to whack a client. Not that that bastard didn't deserve it. Do you know what he threatened to do, I mean *before*? Well, that's a matter for the partners, the management committee in London.'

'Does that mean he'll be forgiven?'

'Don't be ridiculous. I've got to dismiss him as soon as possible. But I want to do it face to face. I don't want him doing anything stupid. While he's in Japan we're responsible for him. He can have a week to pack and go home. Now, don't you think you should tell me why?'

I shrugged.

'Woman trouble?'

'I don't think so.'

'No, he never struck me as the sort to have woman trouble . . . Not . . . well . . . *man* trouble?' Vickers, as he said this, raised his eyebrows at his own suggestion. Then emitted a clenched-teeth laugh. 'No, that I could never imagine, though you have to be open to all possibilities these days . . . No, that at least is beyond the powers of the human imagination. He was never one for most of life's rich tapestry.'

'No.'

'Did he fall in with a bad lot? Some of those merchant wankers—'

'No,' I said.

'You're sure it wasn't woman trouble?'

'Well,' I said. 'I suppose that could have played a part.'

'Really?' He leaned forward a little; a sudden riffle of interest had passed through the lines of that shrewd Lancastrian face whose lineaments our more nervous clients always found so reassuring.

'He did have a girlfriend, Harry,' I conceded.

'Do you have her number? Can we contact her?'

'It's no to both I'm afraid.'

Vickers paused but his curiosity won out. 'What's she like?'

'Everyone asks that.'

'Yes, but – is she the reason?'

'I don't know. It's an . . . unusual relationship.'

'I sometimes think,' said Vickers, in what I took to be an oblique reference to Mrs Vickers, 'that all relationships are unusual.' He briefly shared his tired smile with me. 'Pretty girl, is she?'

'Yes.'

'I've often wondered,' said Vickers, 'to be honest, what it would be like, going out with one of the local girls . . .' This unforeseen interlude in his usual routine appeared to have made him reflective. It was one of those moments when things quieten, the impersonal rush subsides, and a person seems to come properly into focus for the first time. 'Still.' Once again he shared his special tired smile with me. 'Whatever the reason, we need him out of our hair and back in England. ASAP. Clients don't pay £175 an hour to be biffed on the nose, do they? . . . Anyway, we've' – he didn't explain who *we* were – 'we've had a word with the landlord. One of his boys will let you in. If he's there, I want you to get the idiot over here. If he's not, I want you to, well, to go through the flat. Check he doesn't have any papers or other property of the firm there. Who knows what he's been up to? I don't want anything sensitive left lying around.'

'Is that legal?' I asked.

'Look, we rent the fucking thing. And for a fucking fortune. So just please do it, OK. Thank you. For heaven's sake.'

'Am I authorized to look in pockets?'

'Look, just get on with it, will you.' He made a flapping but good-humoured gesture with his hand, thereby dismissing me.

I stood up, and was at the door when Vickers called me back.

I looked round. 'Sorry?'

'He wouldn't, well, kill himself, would he?'

'No. I don't think so.'

'Anyway, let me know what you find. I have to ring London once they wake up. Now, off you go, *please*.'

After the man at reception had insisted there'd been no sightings, the landlord's representative took me up in the lift. There were treacly streaks in his hair and he exercised gum steadily. When the lift opened on Meadowlark's floor, he clicked his fingers. A loud sharp snap. I'd no idea why. Maybe he thought of it as Esperanto for *Here we are*, having little English. I spoke to him in Japanese. The landlord, it turned out, was his uncle. The job was boring, but not as boring as school. His ambition was to be a DJ. He plucked disdainfully at his suit. When his mates saw him in it, they mocked him as a sell-out. He was interested in Meadowlark. In his uncle's office, it seemed, Meadowlark was already a legendary figure. My escort wished he'd seen him. How big was he really? Twice your height, I assured him. He gave me a playful nudge with his elbow, but was careful not to connect, then pulled out a clogged ring of keys. I listened to him chew while he picked over the cluster of options. The door responded to his third choice and opened with a loud pop. He gave it a violent shove and it slammed back against the side wall. He walked straight in, showing no fear of meeting the legendary Meadowlark's ghost.

The rooms all had the same stale aroma of abandonment. We passed quickly from one to the next: living-room, kitchenette, bathroom, bedroom. There was no body, just a sad, scattered corpus of possessions, evidence of a hasty, half-thought-out departure. I checked the wardrobe. It was solid with dark, capacious suits.

'Well, he hasn't been head-hunted.'

I closed the door on them and looked back at the unmade bed. The drawer beside it had been dragged out. Meadowlark must have scrabbled in there for whatever items he deemed essential for his flight.

Suddenly music was booming all around me. I stepped back into the living-room. The treacle-haired nephew was crouched before Meadowlark's matt black stereo, know-ledgeable fingers experimenting with the controls. Young male Japanese voices rose in anodyne harmony, then were rudely silenced. The nephew turned his head. I could see he was both puzzled and amused.

'He *likes* SMAP?'

'He's a big fan.'

'People *like them* in England?'

'Oh yes. Bigger than the Beatles.'

'No.' He stood, grinning. His teeth were nicotine-stained.

'My sister went to see them and pissed herself . . . Your friend isn't gay, is he?'

'You're the second person to ask me that today.'

'Well, the girls all think they're cute. I don't like Japanese bands. *All shit*,' he added, in English.

'What about KoKo Wanabe?' I said. 'He's a big fan of hers also.'

'This guy is strange,' said the treacle-haired nephew. 'I never thought a lawyer would listen to that kind of music.'

Recalling that I was supposed to be searching – drawers, and also pockets – I went back into the bedroom and reopened the wardrobe. It was strange to think that Meadowlark and Sachiko had stood naked together in this very room. I started slipping my hand into pockets: jacket pockets, trouser pockets, back pockets, breast pockets. They felt dank, unpleasantly gritty at the bottom. I doubted that any of the suits had been cleaned in a long time. Eventually I found a small, clumsily folded orange card. I knew what that was without having to look. I pocketed it and resumed, my sense of anticipation sharpened by this modest but important discovery. But nothing else turned up apart from a few coins. Meadowlark, it appeared, was an assiduous emptier of pockets. I turned round to reconsider the rest of the bedroom. Then I realized what had been pressing, half-formed, at the back of my mind. I strode back into the living-room. Yes, both portraits were gone. The space was icon-free. He'd abandoned his suits but not his monarch.

The nephew was now sprawled on Meadowlark's sofa. He looked bored. I went into the kitchenette and opened the cupboards. Glass whose source wasn't immediately clear crunched softly like sand underfoot. A well-stuffed bin liner, loosely knotted by its own neck, rested against the oven. A faint, unpleasant smell hung over it. I crouched down and untied it. The full stench swept up into my face. I hesitated. My task, presumably, included sifting Meadowlark's refuse. So I peeled on the red washing-up gloves that lay in the sink, rolled up my sleeves and hunkered down again, my clad hands looking simultaneously clinical and flamboyant. The smell was strong, rich, deeply repellent. One man's waste. Nevertheless my nostrils began, slowly, to acclimatize. I gingerly inserted my gloved fingers into the mulch, Meadowlark's compost, dug down gradually between slimy cartons, torn-up packaging, ripped and saturated pages from the *Japan Times*; I slid my arm in deeper, foraging beneath bunched-up balls of kitchen paper whose secret contents I decided to leave intact, the flabby skins of fruit, rotted vegetables, plastic bottles, compacted beer cans (compacted presumably by Meadowlark's own hand), then made contact with a hard right-angle which I held and pulled, sliding it up from the bulging belly of the bag, realizing as I did so that it was one of the missing frames, its glass cobwebbed by fissures and cracks. I saw the smeared top of the photograph, a stiff wave of hair, then left it lodged there and reached back down. I felt – near the bottom – the rectilinear shape of the other frame, then part of what I thought was a playing card, which I brought to the surface instead, and turned over. It was one half of a photograph, ripped straight down so as to neatly bisect its subject, an unsmiling, fully clothed Sachiko. I found the solitary eye staring out at me unexpectedly unsettling. I left it on the floor and went digging for the rest of her. I felt several candidates, and began to draw them out, one by one, half by half, all identically torn – he must have dealt with the whole pack of photos in one moment of abrupt, angry force. Using my forefinger I wiped them down before matching them on the floor. Sachiko's eyes were reunited and lost their perplexing percipience. Her head was restored to its torso in two vertical shots. They appeared to comprise a sequence, neither her sulky expression nor her dress changing. I plumbed the mulch again, then slowly withdrew, sticky unidentified objects detaching themselves from the skin of my forearm as I did so.

I opened my hand. The blotched Japanese girl smiling up at me was not Sachiko. I had never seen her before. She was not as pretty. In fact she was rather plain, her face somewhat square-shaped. The eyes were rounder than Sachiko's and there were discreet auburn highlights in her hair. She seemed about the same age, maybe a year or two older. There was, I thought, something strangely hopeful, perhaps even a little scared, about her smile. The fragment terminated, roughly, at her bare neck. I dug down to retrieve her shoulders and bust. I never found the rest of her body but I did find two more of her face, both times with the same expression. I paused and stood to rinse clean the silted glove, then began again. Down my hand went. I found a pair of crossed, miniskirted legs cut off at the waist and then Sachiko, one arm raised, flaring, annoyed. I imagined Meadowlark behind his camera, despairing of ever coaxing out a smile. After that I retrieved just one more torn half, as poorly composed as the others, with only a cheek, a sliver of face and the very corner of an eye visible. It was certainly not Sachiko. I compared it with the other girl, holding them both up to the light, but could not decide.

The nephew appeared in the doorway while I was standing at the sink, scrubbing my hands and forearms under the tap. He came over and looked down at the fragmentary photographs where I'd spread them out beside the micro-wave, two dozen cold traces of Meadowlark's previously unknown home life. He pored over each one with great interest, murmuring to himself as he did so. I sensed that Meadowlark was being rehabilitated in his eyes.

'I'm sorry,' I said, turning off the tap. 'There were no spring pictures.' Then, deciding I might as well take advantage of his native expertise, I separated off the sliver of anonymous face and the images of the unknown girl. He wasn't sure at first, going through them several times, lifting up each fragment and angling them to compare. Finally he reached a verdict. It was someone else. Another, third, face.

'I see your friend is a collector,' said the landlord's nephew.

# 14

## MOSHI MOSHI

'*Moshi moshi?*'

'Hi,' I said in English.

'Hello?' she answered doubtfully.

'Don't you remember me?' I asked in Japanese.

'Who is this?' She stuck to English. 'Who speaking?'

'Don't you remember me?'

'No.'

I enlightened her.

'Oh,' she said, without enthusiasm. 'What you want?'

I asked after Meadowlark.

There was a pause. This silence, rather than her words, helped me to picture her. I saw her eyes, thin, suspicious, two dark slashes, as she thought what to say, her little tensed hand tightening its grip on her treasured mobile.

'Do you know where he is?' I said in English.

'No.'

'Doesn't he telephone you anymore?'

'No.'

'Are you sure?'

'I put down.'

'You mean you won't speak to him?'

'No.'

'Why?'

'I don't want see.'

'Will you see me?'

'No.'

'I'm trying to find him.'

'Yes, find him.' Her impatient voice implied a brief, dismissive gesture.

'But can you help me?'

'No.'

'So you won't see me?'

'No.'

'But I want to give you something.'

Sachiko paused.

'I want to give you something,' I repeated.

'What?' Her voice was sharp. She wanted to know, but resented this appeal to her curiosity. 'What thing?'

'Something I found.'

'Found?'

'In his flat.'

Now it was my turn to pause. I let her mind turn. I knew she was trying to remember. Frowning to herself as she ransacked her memory. It didn't help her.

'What thing?' she demanded once again.

'Nothing really. Just some photographs. Would you like them back?'

'Where find?'

'I said. His flat. We've got the keys now.'

'All?'

'I suppose so.'

'*What*?'

'Yes, all of them.'

'Give me.' Her voice was suddenly tight.

I now took a chance that the photographs hadn't stopped at the point I'd reached in my search. I looked down at her soiled orange card where it lay on my desk. 'There's some nice ones of the two of you.'

'*You see?*'

'Well, I had to look to know I'd found them.'

'*Private.*' Anger and frustration vibrated together in her voice. '*Private thing.*'

'So would you like them?'

'Give me,' she pleaded. I thought I heard her hit something. Maybe the wall of her little bedroom one hour and thirty minutes by packed train from where I was sitting with my computer purring in front of me. 'Give me.' Again I thought I heard her hit out. I puckered the mouth of the oblong envelope and joggled torn halves of photographs out across my desktop. I subtracted those of the second girl and the unknown sliver of face. 'Give me today,' Sachiko was insisting in my ear. 'Today.' I hesitated over the crossed, miniskirted legs. The miniskirt was pink.

'Do you have a pink miniskirt?' I asked her.

'What?'

'It's for your own good.'

'What?'

I asked her in Japanese.

'No,' she said, surprised.

'Thank you. That's all I need to know.'

I added it to the second pile I'd made on my desk. Her surprise had silenced her and lasted while I deposited this second pile in a second envelope. I scrawled the letter S on the first envelope.

'Hello,' I said. 'Still there?'

'Yes,' she answered, almost meekly, allowing me the initiative.

'I'll meet you,' I said, 'in the McDonald's in Omotesando. Tonight. What will you be wearing?'

'What?'

'Will I recognize you? It's been so long.'

'I am the same,' she said.

She was sitting alone near the far wall, husbanding a milkshake and smoking. This was a new interest. She looked older I thought, even though it was only six weeks since I'd last seen her. Perhaps worry aged her. I could see that she was worried. In the short time she'd been waiting for me she'd already built a small, dirty cairn of cigarette butts. Neither her personal organizer nor her mobile phone was visible.

I raised a hand to indicate I'd seen her – she didn't respond, just smoked and blankly gazed in what could have been my direction – then queued at the counter to buy a coffee before crossing the restaurant to join her. Her hair was tied back and she was dressed entirely in innocent white: white trainers, white jeans, a blank white T-shirt, like a beguiling empty space waiting to be filled in. A white puffa jacket had been hooked by its shoulders to the neighbouring chair. Only the thin black stripe of her belt and the shiny anthracite of her hair counterbalanced this angelic arrangement. A small plastic carrier bag had been folded over beside her milkshake.

'How are you, Sachiko?' I asked, squeezing in opposite her.

'OK.' She smoked and considered me sourly.

'We don't know where he is, but we have to find him.'

'Why?'

'Well, they, my firm, want to sack him. *Fire* him . . . As

soon as possible. And send him home. It could be very embarrassing for them if he does anything stupid. In Japan, that is. Once he's back home, then it's a different matter . . . And anyway, I'd like to see him.'

'Why?'

'He's my friend.'

'Is he?'

'Yes. I'm worried about him.'

'Are you?' She pressed the cigarette into the ashtray, placing what remained after this on the cairn. 'He doesn't like you,' she added, in Japanese. Then, with a look of satisfaction, she drew out a fresh cigarette.

'When he rings you next time, I want you to arrange a meeting. An appointment. And then call me.'

She pulled on the cigarette, then switched to the straw of the milkshake, her other hand holding its base. I watched the thin tube suddenly darken as she drew the sweet sludge up into her mouth. Cigarette smoke lazily unfolded between us. I waited until she raised her head to again exchange pleasures, moving the cigarette back to her puckered lips.

'When did you start smoking?'

'Don't remember . . . Show me photos now.'

'How's your grandfather?'

'He always complaining.' She broke off for another studiedly collected drag on her cigarette. 'He make me tired.'

A commotion behind us distracted her. A group of smiling young women, OLs, were detaching themselves from two nearby tables, clutching expensive handbags, buttoning jackets, smoothing down demure skirts, some giving little fluttery waves, others half-bows to those remaining, who were frantically waving back, the two

groups chorusing to each other in English *bye bye! bye bye!*,
their voices uniformly soprano.

'Well, everyone complains when they're old,' I said.

*bye bye! bye bye!*

'My father took my clothes.' She pronounced it *closes*.

'He took them?'

*bye bye! bye bye!*

'He said I have too many for young girl. He throw them
away.' She abruptly moved her hand, scattering ash, her
expression incredulous. 'Shouting, throwing . . . He was
jealous.'

'Jealous?'

'Because I have nice closes.'

'And he doesn't?'

She smiled. Slightly, bleakly. 'All shit. Polyester suit.
Nothing good quality. Cannot afford. My father wear very
bad always. I hate him.'

She lowered her mouth to draw slowly on her milkshake.

'So he threw them away?'

She looked up.

'He throw my Gucci and my Prada and my Paul Smith
and my Chanel.' I could see how even now she was seized
with disbelief. 'He was crazy.' She briefly smoked as she
recalled this dark inexplicable moment of craziness. The
recollection animated her. 'I said, I said — you can't, it's
Chanel, you can't . . . Crazy. Crazy. I was crying. Shouting.'
She talked as if she were describing a younger now distant
self.

'What did you do?'

'Now I keep in other place. He don't know.'

'You mean your closes?'

'Yes. I keep in secret place. I have new things. He don't

know.' Looking sly, she finished with her cigarette and twisted it to a burst lump against the base of the ash tray. Then her eyes were focusing again on my face. 'Show me photos now.'

'I'm sorry. I forgot them,' I said.

For a moment she simply stared. Then she understood. '*Where?*'

'Don't worry. No one else will see them.'

'Where are?' she demanded.

'After I see him, you can have them.'

'Give me now.'

'Uh-uh.'

'*Mine. They're mine!*' I could see she was about to cry.

'Sorry.'

She looked down at the tabletop. Her straight black fringe hid her eyes.

'I didn't want to,' she said quietly.

'I'm sorry?'

'Do them. Pictures. Didn't want.'

She fumbled out the last cigarette from the sleek, crested packet, her face strangely wrinkled around the mouth.

'Let me.'

Her lighter was unexpectedly heavy. I inspected it. A platinum shell capped in gold. Its blue flame stroked the filter-tip into orange life. She pulled. Then sweetened her mouth with the revivifying milkshake, drawing on the straw at length. Her pale face slowly calmed.

I returned the lighter. 'New?'

'Present,' she said. 'From friend.'

'If only my friends were as generous. Your friends must like you very much.'

'Yes,' she said. 'They do.'

'Why?'

'Because I'm nice person.' She blew smoke. 'And cute.'

'How's KoKo Wanabe?'

'She has new CD. I will get tomorrow.'

'And a new book of salacious photos?'

'No. No book.'

'How's her boyfriend?'

'They going to get married.'

'When?'

'No one know. Maybe after next *basho*.'

'Don't you think it's dangerous,' I asked, 'making love with a sumo wrestler?'

'I don't know,' she said seriously. 'Maybe she go on top.' She puffed and thought about this.

'Must do,' I agreed. 'KoKo's such a fragile-looking girl.'

'What is frag-ile?'

'Weak. Easily broken. Not strong.'

'No.' Sachiko shook her head. 'KoKo Wanabe very strong . . . Always very strong girl,' she repeated, certain on this point.

She dipped her face and gargled up the last of the milkshake. She kept pulling on the straw, long-lashed eyes downcast, until fully satisfied it was empty. Then she announced, standing as she did so, 'Go toilet . . . Come back.'

She walked away, looking around with superior interest at the other tables, so defiantly *together*, buttocks two neat little parcels in the tight grip of her lunar white trousers, her soft handbag with its gold clasp clamped in a businesslike hand.

When she'd gone I used a sly forefinger to fidget open the carrier bag she'd left on the table. Inside was a block of

Winnie-the-Pooh writing paper and a packet of matching envelopes, both cellophane-wrapped. I withdrew my finger and the opening curled shut again. A few minutes later Sachiko returned and slid back onto her chair.

She looked at her milkshake. 'Buy me another,' she said, the command delivered in a bare hard voice which long ago lost interest in the padding of coquetry.

'Why?' I asked. 'Why should I buy you a milkshake?'

'I'm thirsty,' she explained.

I stood and crossed to the counter. I bought her a strawberry milkshake. She sampled it.

'I wanted chocolate,' she complained.

'I thought you always drank strawberry.'

'I changed.'

I remained standing. 'So you know what to do?'

'Yes,' she said eventually, holding the base of her new drink. 'Yes, if he calls.'

## SACHIKO'S DEPARTURE

'I go now,' said Sachiko. She snapped open her handbag and slid out her mobile. She called up a stored number. 'I'm finished,' she told someone in Japanese.

I watched her walk outside. Shortly after a silver BMW – a foreign car, a rare sight – slowed to a smooth halt just in front of the McDonald's. The driver was wearing a peaked cap and grey jacket. There was no one else inside. He climbed out and opened the rear door, lowering his head politely as he did so to the slim, petite girl in white waiting on the kerbside. Sachiko stepped in with the oblivious assurance vouchsafed by familiarity. He could have been collecting the boss's daughter.

# 15

I sat on my sofa spooning up yoghurt, watching the earnest American breakfast news on cable. There'd been earth tremors in the neighbouring Kansai region overnight strong enough to do damage, and the camera panned from a hazy distance several listing and collapsed houses and a small, plaintive hillock of debris. Ten or twelve people had been injured. We glimpsed the bare dirty feet of one of them as he was bounced away on a stretcher. It was not an incident of any significance. It was something which happened from time to time.

I'd first experienced such a tremor, though milder, on my second flight into Japan two years before, as I stood blearily in line at passport control. It was an impressive hall – high-ceilinged, imperial. Then, without warning, a subterranean force had moved through the floor. Tidal, inexorable, an immense swell and surge of hidden power. The momentary flexing (I'd thought) of a buried giant just below one's feet. It had been too modest a tremor to merit comment. None of the Japanese around me had even paused in what they were doing.

But I knew that in 1923 the great Kanto earthquake had levelled Tokyo and its environs, had casually shivered it to a landscape of human scarecrows, ruins and scree. One hundred and forty thousand people had died. Everyone I passed in the street that morning on my way to work carried, at some level, a folk memory of that day within them. They might build higher and higher (and deeper and deeper), with ever more layered office space and apartments, airborne highways proliferating, packing in more and more power lines and suited bodies, but eventually that dormant giant, buried out of sight for so long, would not merely shift his corpus in its periodic restlessness but begin, early one innocuous morning, without fanfare or warning, to rise to his knees, his feet, bursting through the surface in a million different places. But still we streamed across the great crossroads in our orderly human waves, anxious to resume where we'd left off the night before.

My telephone rang while I was doing work for Mr Kanazawa, our exciting new client. A seventy-seven-year-old peasant who'd had the foresight to buy up charred swathes of firebombed Tokyo shortly after the war ended, he was now interested in cutting himself a thick slice of balustraded central London (where the ground never, inconveniently, moved).

'Hello there.' It was Harvey. 'There's a lull on the floor. So thought I'd give you a ring.'

'That was kind.'

'What you doing?'

'Drafting,' I said. 'I love drafting in the morning.'

'Is it really worth it?'

'I'm sorry?'

'For the money I mean. For what you get.'

'I survive.'

'Shit money though, isn't it? Our in-house guy does much better.'

'And you do better than him.'

'I suppose so. I saw our mutual friend.'

'That why you're phoning?'

'Yeah. I know you're all looking for him.'

'Where?'

'Ikebukuro.'

'Was he alone?'

'You mean was he with a woman?'

'No, was he alone?'

'Yeah . . . He looked very alone.'

'You spoke to him?'

'Well, he was busy.'

'Busy?'

'I nodded though. Smiled.'

'When was this?'

'This morning. About three hours ago. Anyway, gotta go. Give him a hug from me.'

I e-mailed Vickers. *Houston, we have contact.*

Thirty seconds later the jaunty bars of the Camptown Races heralded his reply.

*Eh?*

I tried again, sending my reply-reply.

*Thar she blows!*

My telephone rang. Vickers's Mancunian tones had always struck me as somehow deeply *inapposite* in Tokyo. Too human, I suppose. He sounded amused. 'What're you on about?'

'There's been a sighting.'

'Well stop arsing around and tell me about it.'

I told him.

'Go over and see if he's still there.'

'What about Mr Kanazawa's contract?'

'Look, just fucking go over there,' repeated Vickers amiably. 'God give me strength.'

I took a taxi as I wasn't paying. Watching the white-gloved hands make surgical adjustments to the wheel as we negotiated the great crossroads and boulevards of central Tokyo, I wondered if the story of Meadowlark's violent removal of just such a pair had now circulated and acquired the status of legend in the cab-driving world. The foreign giant who forcibly exposes our hands. Then I saw the driver's eyes in the rear-view mirror – he'd caught me looking at him or, rather, at his gloves. I glanced away. *Yes, he was no doubt thinking, these foreigners who come here are strange. Even when they live here, like this one obviously does, they remain so bizarre and strange.*

Ikebukuro that morning was gripped by endless columns of shoppers, stubbornly coiling and uncoiling. We cut across the massed, angry traffic, skirted the long concrete side of Seibu Department Store. I disembarked. The crowds here were dowdier, more cheaply dressed than in Ginza or Roppongi. I slipped between a line of foreign street vendors, their backs to the railings, proffering trays of glittering trinkets to the passers-by. Meadowlark, unsurprisingly, was not among them offering his own drawer of cut-price ornaments, but I asked after him. A white, Slavic-sounding man, head piled up with crusted dreadlocks, and his harassed-looking girlfriend thought they'd seen him. Or someone like him. But not here. This was in Shinjuku. Where they also hawked their little tray of jumbled trinkets. The strained face of the girlfriend became more strained as she tried to remember for me. I repeated my list of distinguishing characteristics. They didn't (as I might have) laugh. Briefly they discussed together their possible sighting, using their stiff, unsyncopated English instead of lapsing into Polish or Czech or whatever they spoke, out of deference to me. Nearby an old Japanese man with pitted skin and incomplete teeth was selling purple sweet potatoes from a barrow. He could have been standing there in 1948, looking exactly the same, but for his technicolour U2 sweat-shirt. I went over.

'I like U2,' I told him in Japanese as I paid for three potatoes. 'Great band.'

'Who?' he grunted as steam uncurled around us. 'Who?'

While we ate, a woman shopper briefly clucked over the Slavic couple's trinkets, prodding at the things, unimpressed. She asked them rapid questions about quality and country of origin which they couldn't understand, continuing to pick and finger while they smiled haplessly at her. Finally, to our collective relief, she chose a tiny pair of droplet earrings after pressing them hard against her lobes and squinting ferociously from different angles into the small square of mirror they held in front of her.

'Our first sale today,' said the man.

'Yes, you bring us luck,' smiled his girlfriend.

But the woman was coming back, shaking her head and muttering, holding up one earring. It had snapped in two. I watched while they reimbursed her.

'Sorry,' I said. 'It's the lawyer's curse. I'd better move on.'

I joined the human traffic, following its curving route around the great dark hulk of Seibu Department Store, eating the crumbled remains of my sweet potato off a cupped hand as I walked.

It was good not to work. To just walk and watch and eat hot sweet potato off my palm and fingers while enjoying the secret pleasures of the idling spectator. Though I knew it was considered most impolite, indeed vulgar, to eat and walk in this way. But then I was just a *gaijin* who could know no better, and would therefore be indulged. I passed a McDonald's. I had spent my first ever New Year's Day in Japan downstairs in that very outlet, sitting alone and depressed, encircled by tables of middle-aged housewives overseeing their daughters, the girls brilliant in sumptuous holiday kimonos, like a clustering of excited ladies of the ancient, long-lost court or floating world, their young voices chirruping from all directions around the solitary, un-explained white man while they gripped and bit into bulging, sagging hamburgers and pulled at card wallets of grease-slick fries. I'd thought the kimonos far too beautiful for that subterranean plastic world. But for them there was no contradiction. It was a foreigner's contradiction only.

Just ahead of me as I walked, in among the black hair of the marching shoppers, was a slow-moving, broad-shouldered chicken, square placard aloft, its legend pro-claiming the indubitable deep-fried attractions of KRAZEE CHICKEN.

I moved to pass it, glancing up as I did.

'Hello there stranger,' I said.

He wasn't pleased to see me. He stopped abruptly; simply stood there, saying nothing, while the single-minded crowd streamed around us. One brown-gloved hand rose to toy needlessly with his livid crest.

'Are you a cock or a hen?' I asked.

Meadowlark didn't speak. His heavy face bore no dis-cernible expression.

'Love the plumage,' I said.

He turned away from me.

'You ran out of money?'

The chicken's vast high back seemed to be rippling. I thought he might be crying. But he kept his face hidden from me, and I couldn't be sure.

'Look,' I said. 'There's no disgrace in being a chicken.'

I tugged gently at the feathers but still he wouldn't turn. He'd lowered the placard; his crested head was bowed. I could see, between his splayed feet, the weak shadow of his beak.

'We all have to dress up for work,' I persisted. 'I'm also in a costume I didn't choose.'

Meadowlark slowly swung round. There was an unfamiliar bloodiness in his eyes.

'Why did you run off?'

'I don't know,' he said eventually. 'I wasn't feeling well.'

'Where are you staying?'

'In a *gaijin* house.'

'What, four to a room, one stove between thirty?'

'It's okay.'

'Wouldn't you be better off just going home?'

'I don't know,' he said.

'Have you contacted your parents? Harry's bound to if you don't.'

He said nothing.

'Harvey spotted you.'

'I know . . . I could have killed him.'

'Odd to find him here in the morning.'

'No doubt his prick had something to do with it.'

'Probably,' I said. 'Want to go in there?'

There was a small glum coffee shop immediately behind

us. As I spoke, its automatic door slid open and two smiling women stepped out, one with a po-faced child mounted in traditional style on her back.

'Don't think I want to pay four hundred yen for a coffee today.'

'It's on me.'

Wind ruffled the bloodbright cockscomb. 'Gosh, you're so warm and considerate.' I didn't like the way KRAZEE CHICKEN's tallest bird was now looking at me.

'We can catch a cab to my place if you prefer. Talk there.'

He thought about this new proposal, absently pushing up his glasses as they began to edge their way down the broad scarp of his nose.

'Come on.' I tugged at his feathery flank. And, surprisingly, he came, allowing me to pull him gently towards the kerb without a word. Three taxis slowed, then changed their minds, but the fourth one I flagged was willing to take a chance on the two *gaijin* and we crawled in, leaving the placard to work alone, propped against the railings.

In the taxi, leaning forward to avoid repeated collisions of his crown against the roof, Meadowlark picked free the chicken gloves and then peeled off the crested head. And I saw, for the first time, as his own head emerged, how he'd had it shaven, its size brutally magnified by this new, uncompromising nakedness. The spectacles which clung on doggedly to his face looked suddenly tinny and implausible, incapable of domesticating what had been so savagely scalped and revealed.

I whistled. 'Nice haircut.'

'Yes,' murmured Meadowlark, looking out the window. 'It makes children cry.'

I studied the way his field of stubble tapered to a neat arrowhead just above the bulging cylinder of his neck.

'No, it really does,' he continued, almost pressing his ridged nose to the glass as rain began to dab and blear its surface and, across the craggy, canyon-riven face of Tokyo a million umbrellas uniformly flowered. 'I sat down in Mister Donut and the toddler at the next table started to cry.'

'What did you do?'

'I smiled and winked at him. That really got him going.' Now the rain was hammering like a thousand vengeful toddlers on the roof, striping the window through which Meadowlark continued to peer. 'I was asked to leave.'

'By who?'

'The manager. The mother complained. She was quite right to. Why should she have to put up with strange foreigners?' We had halted, locked in a column of cars whose extremities were lost in the haze of the downpour. Meadowlark's fingers were drumming on the pane in time to the greater drumming outside. 'I like it,' he added, in a voice somehow in sympathy with the misty rain. 'It's honest . . . That's what I asked for. An honest haircut.'

'There's certainly something priestlike about it.'

'I did think of that . . . trying a monastery for a while. They say the Buddhists welcome *gaijin*.' His irritating tattoo on the glass continued to mimic the impact of the rain. I wasn't sure he was even aware he was doing it, aware of his fingers' urgent, obsessive dance. 'I had it done' – his other hand touched his head – 'in Kyoto. On my first day. I was there for a week. There were too many temples.' We had started moving again. Horns complained pointlessly around us as if there was a culprit. 'Too many shrines . . . The priests just seem to spend their time lounging around smoking . . .'

'You couldn't possibly stop that?' I said.

'What?' He sounded, I thought, almost sleepy.

'That drumming with your fingers.'

'Is it irritating you?' He could have been asking me if I believed in the Divine or some other metaphysical principle. There was no relaxing of that self-absorbed, glassy beat, as if it was nothing to do with my request. 'I saw the Gold Pavilion . . . I read a student monk burnt it down because it was too perfect. Too beautiful.' The rain had slackened to a sullen drizzle. The passing pavements and dull façades of stained brick and concrete, their roofs speared with aerials, shone wetly.

I knew the story of the mad student but I let him meander on.

Finally I interrupted. 'Do you want to go home?'

'I don't know.' We were in Roppongi now. In the dreary aftermath of the rain it had a shut-down, switched-off look, its dozens of hidden bars waiting, I knew, for the neon night and the white men in suits and the microskirted girls with their dark almond eyes. I saw, not far ahead, my building.

Sitting there on my sofa, dominating it, he seemed pliant enough, but I also sensed, just below that, his residual strength – and knew I shouldn't prod too thoughtlessly at his exposed surface. He didn't want coffee. He wanted green tea. 'I've grown to like the bitterness,' he explained.

So I made him green tea. When I came back into the room with the handleless mug burning my skin, he was sprawled with those great feathered knees casually parted, the fingers of one hand drumming on the armrest (just as they had on the taxi window). Under his breath he was humming, quite fiercely I thought.

'Come on, come on,' he suddenly urged me. 'Chop chop. Chop chop.' And then he was stretching forward to take the mug with its fetching, pale blue bamboo design, the listing, knuckled stalks so delicately drawn, clustering together, taking it with his palm and fingertips, holding it tightly, not even appearing to register the thing's intense heat. Certainly I saw no hint of even a suppressed reaction anywhere across the newly expanded Meadowlark face (expanded by the mowing off of all his hair). Just as the ear-lier shame of discovery (had he really turned his back to hide from me muffled, staccato sobs?) had also gone, en-abling him to sprawl so confidently, suddenly reborn as the lord of my dismal little living-room.

'How long've you been doing that?' I indicated his costume.

'Coupla days.' The energetic fingers of the mug-free hand maintained their tempo. 'Think it's good for me.'

'Why?'

'The humiliation,' said Meadowlark, as if the point were obvious. 'It's good for me.' His fingers seemed now to be drumming with increasing force.

'Really?'

'This is only the beginning,' said Meadowlark.

'I see . . . Where'd you get these ideas?'

'Nowhere. I've struck out on my own now.'

'I see.'

He looked, I thought, pleased with himself. 'I didn't like,' he explained, 'what I was becoming.'

'What were you becoming?'

The fingers pursued their relentless solo on the fake

leather of the armrest. He wasn't interested in answering.

'I saw Sachiko,' I said.

'Why?'

'I asked her to help me find you.'

'That . . . person,' said Meadowlark, 'is in need of a lesson.'

'Which you're proposing to teach?'

'Maybe I will . . . Maybe I will. I tell you, it has to stop,' he added, obscurely.

'Aren't you forgetting her age?'

'If I told you everything,' said Meadowlark, 'if I . . .'

'Why don't you?'

'Oh you'd like that. If I told you everything . . .' He drank, then grimaced wetly, redly.

'Not bitter enough?'

Ignoring me, he finished the tea in five or six great gulps, bulbous droplets clinging to his lips, but continued to hold the mug with the same centripetal force.

'Want something else? A beer?'

He shook his head.

'You no longer drink beer?'

'No. Finished with all that.'

'Because your body is a temple?'

But now his gaze was busy ranging over my living-room, its humdrum miscellany of possessions.

'I know what you're going to say,' I said.

'What?'

'I happen to be attached to my hi-fi.'

'And your TV.'

'Definitely that. I need it like a narcotic.'

'I know.' He stood. 'So he's still here.'

'Who?'

He was pointing at my monochrome picture of Dazai

Osamu, balancing on a stool in Lupin's Bar in Ginza in 1947, dressed in Western shirt and waistcoat, dark hair tangled, his handsome face with its dissolute cheekbones smiling mysteriously at both of us – no, away from us.

'Yes,' I said. 'He's still here.'

Then suddenly Meadowlark was striding across my room, filling it as he did so, and, just as suddenly, he was at the wall and the picture (attached with Blu-Tak) had been snapped free, was in his hands (the mug with its delicate, clustering bamboo left abandoned, on its side, against a caster) and he was tearing it, tearing Dazai, the first time right through the face, separating one high cheekbone from the other, dividing the shrewd, amused eyes, and then he was tearing it crossways, then doubling the scraps so he could tear them again.

Abruptly he stopped.

'Have you finished?' I asked.

We listened together to his breathing. He was gasping for breath.

'What exactly is the point you're making?'

He brandished the scraps at me. He was still panting from his exertion.

'I thought your body was a temple nowadays.'

'I may not, I may not,' he began, 'really know who this person was other than that he wrote a lot of books, words, you'll never be able to properly understand and that he killed himself for reasons I have no knowledge of but which seem to impress you but I don't think you've any right, any right to have his picture on your wall what's he to you or you to him you've never taken a risk a chance and you never will you cling to your shitty job and this shitty flat and watch everyone just watch everyone and that's really all you do. Isn't it?'

'Arguably,' I said.

'So I've torn him up for you, just as I tore her up – in here.' He touched his crown. 'You know, there was a time I even thought I'd have to go to Thailand . . . to fuck her out of my system.'

'Pardon?' I said.

'You heard . . . Anyway, what would you know about that?' He was walking away from the wall he'd assaulted, letting fragments of my *poète maudit* slip from his hands. They left a trail across the carpeted floor.

## RISIBLE SUGGESTIONS

When, later, I suggested he come with me to the office, come to see Vickers, *get it all over with*, he refused, shaking his great scalped head, quietly – but chidingly – going *tch tch, tch tch*. It was the same when I asked for his address. *Tch tch*, he admonished. *Tch tch*. Two quite risible suggestions (I was left in no doubt).

Half man, half shaggy fowl, he crossed to the door.

'Is this it?' I asked.

'It might be,' he told me sonorously, enigmatically.

'You drink my tea, tear up my picture and then go.'

He fumbled with the lock and handle. He was still clumsy.

I stepped forward. 'It's not locked.'

He left the door half open behind him. Shortly after I heard the whispering approach of the lift. Closing the door, I sat down to telephone Vickers.

# 16

**THE PARTY**

Vickers let me in. It was a long time since I'd been inside his flat. A murmur of voices enfolded in soft classical music was audible through the hallway door. He pushed it – a wide room, turning a corner out of sight, the guests' hair brilliantined by halogen lighting, earnest couples in pockets and spots of shadow. A few faces glanced my way to check up on the new arrival. I took in the lacquered furniture, a sumptuous sofa with armchairs, an arrangement of pale flowers done *ikebana* style in a mottled blue vase. There was glass running the entire length of the wall opposite, spectacularly filled by the red and silver pinpricked upper storeys of night-time Tokyo. I was, once again, both envious and impressed.

'Well, off you go and mingle, lad,' said Vickers, giving me a pat in the small of my back to send me on my way. I smiled at Heather, who'd been cornered most uncomfortably against the near wall by Sanderson. (Reconciled to the firm by a large credit note and two discounted bills.) He'd rested an ostensibly paternal hand on her bare arm to underline some inaudible but doubtless profound observation on the Far Eastern capital markets. It remained there while his liver-dark lips elaborated. I moved on. I hated having to wear a suit and tie in the evening.

Our other partner, Symons, was talking with Mr Kanazawa through Mr Kanazawa's chief aide, Kumamoto, bending confidentially towards the property magnate who was barely five foot tall while Kumamoto, gazing blankly into space ten inches above his boss, cut unemotionally between extended chunks of Japanese (loquacious, over-eager Mr Symons) and brutally concise – if ungrammatical – English (laconic Mr Kanazawa, used to being courted). I was beckoned over by Symons to meet our new tycoon. He looked up at me without even mild interest. I looked down, admiring his pinstriped bespoke suit, his handmade brogues, his painted silk tie pale and delicate as a water-colour. He was oddly muscular, solid of build, for a man of seventy-seven and his face had something of the quality of unglazed clay about it, as if it were friable, his narrow eyes and mouth like three terse afterthoughts hurriedly scraped by his maker into its cracked surface. He was a peasant in a two thousand pound suit (and proud of that fact).

I had no idea how to exchange pleasantries with a stunted, uninterested tycoon of dubious reputation (but then the super-rich attract rumours as a rubbish dump draws flies), an old man who'd once been a penniless labourer and now amused himself between half a dozen homes, who'd been formed as a person seven decades ago when Japan was very different, indeed so different as to have been another country, and who'd bought his first tract of black, burnt ground almost twenty years before I was born. So I told him in Japanese of my plan that year to take up the ancient sport of *kendo*, to don its great, stinking head-guard so I could run, clad entirely in flapping black, ritually shouting, at my opponent and then suffer the arrival of his altogether more artful blade, sudden as a rockfall, against my masked forehead. Mr Kanazawa looked at me. Symons, who had, of course, not understood, was staring. Mr Kanazawa in billing terms represented fifty thousand pounds a year (and rising). And so Symons, because he hadn't understood, stared at us as if something might be in the balance. And then Mr Kanazawa smiled. 'Good luck, young man,' he said (in Japanese). 'Good luck, young man,' said Kumamoto (in English). I briefly nodded my head. It would have been stupid to offer my hand. A still anxious Symons, as if now relieving my slippery fingers of a priceless antique vase, said softly, 'You should go and speak to Professor Tokugawa,' and then, to distract our tycoon, began to fulsomely praise me in English (I was, I learned, hand-picked) while Kumamoto resumed his dreary task of translation.

Tall and greying, Professor Tokugawa, an authority on Japanese and international law, was cheerfully holding court in his elegant English (tinged with a North American inflexion – he'd studied then taught for several years at Princeton). He was something of a pundit, a dabbler in journalism, who was always amiably laughing. 'Yes, yes,' he was saying to two balding English bankers and their English wives, 'my family are of samurai stock. But my father' (smiling, chuckling at the memory for reasons not altogether clear) 'gave all our swords and armour and scrolls to our hometown museum. They were always pestering him for them. So now my family history – alas – is all behind glass. But, maybe we are better off without such baggage. This is, after all, supposed to be a democratic age. Or at least a plutocratic one.' Again there came the familiar warm laugh, a laugh which always made him seem someone irredeemably amused by the arcane complexities of Japanese law he would endeavour on these occasions to patiently unpick for slow-witted English *bengoshi* such as me. (*There are so many of them*, he must have privately thought when talking to me or my colleagues, *like in America, it cannot truly be a profession for the intellectual élite, as here in Japan. There are so many of them. What in the world do they all do?*)

It was then, as a clump of guests near the wall of glass parted, that I saw Sachiko.

Alone, she was gazing out of the window. Silently, thoughtfully, she was admiring the view. It was no hallucination.

Professor Tokugawa was now talking about golf. A popular magazine aimed at housewives had commissioned him to write an article on Japanese Law and the Housewife. 'It is not a particularly large topic,' Professor Tokugawa assured the two glabrous English bankers and their wives. As a sweetener or reward (we learned) for taking on this task, the assistant editor (who was a man, not a housewife) had taken him for a round of golf, that pastime in Japan of the grand and the moneyed. While I watched Sachiko standing motionless before the high, wide glass filled, like an aquarium, with the shimmering upper stories of night-time Tokyo, Professor Tokugawa amused us with his thoughts on the game. 'It's such a foolish activity, certainly for the hamfisted like me.'

I detached myself from the edge of their little group.

'We poor clumsy professors normally entertain ourselves by playing chess and *go*.' He chuckled benignly.

With carpeted stealth, I came up behind her.

'One day,' I said, 'all this will be yours.'

I saw her surprise in her reflection in the glass. My

unpleasantly familiar voice had passed through her like a tremor. Her body petrified. I was the beast who's slipped the latch and crept, without sound or warning, into the secret walled garden. She didn't want me there.

Now Sachiko turned. Stared claret-mouthed at me with a harsh blankness. 'Who are you?' she asked with what she no doubt thought passed for innocence. Her voice was tense, hostile. 'I don't know you. Please go away.'

She had, since I'd last seen her, transformed her appearance. Her eyebrows were gone, replaced by two sharp curves drawn − I thought − with impressive artistry. She'd applied white eyeshadow. I didn't like it. Certain of her nails (I'd noticed her hands, they were stiff, rigid at her sides) had been painted with tiny flowers. Her hair had also changed. It was somehow thicker, more assertive I supposed, and auburn-lightened. It would have been nice to stick both hands in and thoroughly ruffle it. That would have made her squeal and jump.

'What on earth are you doing here?' I asked her.

'*What you?*' she hit back hotly.

'So you do know who I am.'

'No,' she insisted stubbornly. 'Not today.'

'I work for this company. Mr Vickers is one of our partners. This is our client party. What on earth are you doing here?'

'I didn't know name,' she said, looking nervously past me towards the centre of the room.

'Don't worry,' I said. 'Tonight I don't know you . . . But who brought you here?'

'No one,' she said, looking now at the floor, gnawing her wine-red lower lip. I considered this mouth which had once been Meadowlark's domain.

'So you didn't know this was his company?'

'No.'

'Who brought you tonight?'

She lifted her face. 'I am with Mr Kanazawa.'

'You're an item?'

'He is my guardian now.'

'What about Mrs Kanazawa?'

'She old.'

'Doesn't get out much?'

'No,' said Sachiko.

We both paused. Her eyes slid from me to focus again on the centre of the room behind us. She wore, I noted, a short and simple black dress.

'I saw him,' I said. 'About a week ago. He's got a new job. Promoting KRAZEE CHICKEN.'

She didn't smile. I was reminding her of someone now locked away in a determinedly forgotten past.

'What labels are you wearing?' I asked.

'Prada,' she said proudly, perhaps defiantly, eyes still fixed on the scene behind me. 'All Prada.'

'A present from Mr Kanazawa?'

'Yes.'

I heard Vickers's voice. He was calling my name as he approached.

He stopped alongside me, smiling most oddly at Sachiko, at the wine splash of her lips.

'Mr Kanazawa is asking after his young assistant.'

I didn't know why he wouldn't address her directly.

'Thank you,' said Sachiko, prettily bobbing her head. A small anklet winked sweetly as she slipped past us.

'Quite the little doll,' said Vickers, his gaze surreptitiously tracking her as she crossed the floor to the waiting

Kanazawa and Kumamoto. He laughed. 'The dirty old bugger.'

'Yes,' I agreed.

'If you're rich enough, you can go on pulling till the day you die . . . Lucky tosser.'

'She used to go out with Meadowlark,' I said.

'*What? Her?*'

'Oh yes. She's the one.'

Vickers stood there; he was slowly shaking his head, scratching at his scalp (somewhat haplessly I thought), that odd pursed smile once again on his face. 'You're serious?'

'That's the one, Harry.'

'Her and . . .'

'I know,' I said. 'It's hard to imagine.'

He continued to watch Sachiko. She had her back to us now as she talked, inaudibly but busily, to Mr Kanazawa. Kanazawa's expression remained as bleak and uninterested as before. With her heels she was three to four inches taller than him.

'I'm trying to imagine it,' Vickers said. He looked tired, with pouches beneath his eyes (it was as if I'd never noticed them before, perhaps I wasn't used to standing so close to him), his crow's-feet and smile lines suddenly raw and prominent, spreading and radiating even as he rubbed at his eyes. And while we stood together and watched, Mrs Vickers sailed grandly across our line of sight towards the Prada-wrapped object of our attention.

'Christ knows what Maureen's going to make of that girl,' said Vickers.

There was often a crumpled air about Mrs Vickers. It wasn't clear why. Indeed at times she looked more like Harry Vickers's sister than his wife. Her hair was an autumnal folly, an infinitely scalloped burst of russet. A tall, leggy woman in her late forties, she generally favoured trouser suits in unconvincing fruit colours (apricot, lemon, pale melon) but tonight was swishing amongst her guests in a long lime cocktail dress which fully revealed two delicately haired arms and partially revealed a large speckled bust, ideal for pillowing the troubled head of Harry Vickers. As we watched, she docked with her target, grandly shaking hands with each of them in turn. Kumamoto and then Sachiko bowed. The tycoon dipped his head.

'Come on.' Vickers moved to join his wife. I followed.

Mrs Vickers and Mr Kanazawa were exchanging pleasantries while Kumamoto translated. I'd never warmed to her voice. Unlike her husband's, it had a cold Home Counties edge to it, and when I heard it I always thought of hearty women in jodhpurs and jackets, gathering on horseback to watch while frantic hounds turned a struggling fox to ketchup and muscle.

Standing beside Mrs Vickers, more than a head shorter, saying nothing, Sachiko looked very bright and sharp and young.

'I do like Japan,' Mrs Vickers was now telling them without any effort to import conviction. 'I find your culture fascinating.' '*I find your culture fascinating*,' said Kumamoto in Japanese. She looked at Sachiko. 'Have you travelled to the West?'

'No,' said Sachiko. 'I want go Paree. And London. And New York.'

'I'm sure your time will come,' said Mrs Vickers warily.

'Yes,' said Sachiko as if she understood. 'It will.'

Symons now joined us, bringing Professor Tokugawa with him. Another round of introductions ensued. Kumamoto bowed deeply and presented Professor Tokugawa with Mr Kanazawa's card, face up, held out between two hands. Professor Tokugawa bowed less deeply and presented his own card to Mr Kanazawa. Kanazawa briefly dipped his head in response and muttered his ritual appreciation.

Vickers then took it upon himself to introduce Sachiko to the professor. As if on cue, she shrilled a deferential greeting and bowed to the samurai academic with the grand surname as deeply as had Kumamoto. She didn't offer him her card. He was very sweet and courteous in reply, giving her a chivalrously low bow which her status, of course, didn't merit. (I knew he knew exactly – as befitted a pundit – what she was.)

A conversation of sorts then followed. Symons attempted, without success, to spark a dialogue between Mr Kanazawa and the professor. Finally (to salvage what she could) Mrs Vickers stepped in, suggesting that the tycoon come to admire her new painting (a sunset) at the other end of the room. They set off with Kumamoto. Sachiko began to follow but Kanazawa shook his head. One of the English bankers with his wife now drifted over to us.

As if liberated by the tycoon's departure (did he know of those rumours which gathered and circled like flies? had he sensed an entrepreneur's sour suspicion of an academia which never dirties its hands?), Professor Tokugawa flowered once more, and his elegant voice rose again to dominate our reconfigured group. His theme, this time, was generational. So we stood and respectfully listened as he extemporized on the problems between the generations. I noted Symons looking at Vickers. 'Yes, we have problems between the generations,' said Professor Tokugawa, smiling benignly. 'My generation, for all its sacrifices, receives no gratitude at all from our youth. They are far too busy scowling and dyeing their hair.' The professor chuckled. Once again Symons looked at Vickers. But I was happy to listen. Happier to listen to him than to them. 'Well-dressed young women – like young Miss Sachiko here,' continued the professor (Sachiko, face glazed, remote, jerked back to attention, recognizing her name, her curious eyes now on him), 'are even embarrassed nowadays to walk in public alongside their poor salaryman fathers. They think them dirty, unfashionable, shameful.' Professor Tokugawa laughed, smiling to himself at a vision of scented young women shunning their bewildered fathers. 'It's very sad. The salarymen are our backbone – yet even their own daughters despise them. The very fruit of their loins.' We were all impressed by that. This man knew his English. I caught Symons looking once again at Vickers.

I heard a faint sound. It was coming from Sachiko's handbag. I saw her hesitate, then softly click its gold mouth open and half lift out a small, ovoid object whose three tiny buttons she quickly squeezed several times – she didn't need to look, her fingers knew where to press. Then the handbag, just as discreetly, was quietly shut. Her actions had been too fast, too fluent for me to catch sight of the image in the thing's miniature screen. But Professor Tokugawa, as befitted a man with a gimlet eye for social trends, had nevertheless registered those deft movements in and around her little handbag.

'Is that your *tamagotchi*, Miss Sachiko?' he asked in English.

'Yes,' she admitted, reluctantly I thought, unwilling to look us in the eyes.

'How long has it been alive?'

'Five days.' She wouldn't look up.

'Miss Sachiko is nurturing a little chick,' explained the professor. 'Her electronic child. She must feed it, play with it, clean away its waste – so it will grow into a big, healthy bird. If she ignores it when it calls, it will weaken and die.'

'How fascinating,' said the balding banker. 'Could I see?'

'No.' Sachiko sounded alarmed. She gripped her handbag as if the inquisitive Englishman might at any moment yank it from her to satisfy his curiosity.

'Millions have been sold,' continued the social pundit. 'My own daughter, alas, is one of the victims.'

'Really,' said the balding English banker's wife. 'So you allow her to have one?'

'What can I do?' Professor Tokugawa smiled the smile of the helpless, indulgent father. 'It will pass, like everything else. Our fashions here have a very short lifespan, not much longer usually than Sachiko-san's hungry little *tamagotchi*. Probably by next year they will all be in the trash can.'

As he was speaking a new sound suddenly rose from Sachiko's handbag. Her mobile phone, clamouring for attention. 'I'm sorry,' she said in English, then Japanese, giving, as she spoke, an apologetic bow. 'Please excuse.'

She turned away from us, hurriedly fumbling, then bringing the mobile to her ear.

'How old is that girl?' asked the banker's wife.

'I've no idea,' I said.

Sachiko had withdrawn to the unadorned near wall where Sanderson had previously cornered Heather.

'Who is she exactly?' persisted the banker's wife.

'Mr Kanazawa's assistant,' explained Symons. He looked as if he'd been accused of procuring.

'I see,' she said in a voice intended to leave us in no doubt that she really did *see*. 'Not one of those telephone club girls, then?'

'One of those what?' said the glabrous banker.

'Go back to sleep, dear. My husband's too busy making money to have any idea what's going on.'

Professor Tokugawa smiled uncertainly.

'Of course I know what's going on,' objected the banker.

'Yes, darling.'

I glanced back at Sachiko. She'd pressed a hand to her free ear and was talking fast into the phone, one delicate, elegantly heeled foot tapping as she spoke. Its movement became fiercer while I watched, the stiletto tearing at the soft white carpet. Her spare hand had formed a claw. While I watched it began to scrape and scratch at Vickers's unadorned wall. Her voice became louder.

'Is something wrong?' asked the banker.

Symons eyed me.

'I'll check everything's okay,' I said.

Clawing the wall with her nails, talking urgently into the mouthpiece, she didn't at first register my presence. When she ceased speaking, and listened instead, her teeth bit deep into her lower lip.

'Who is it?'

She lifted one shoulder, as if needing shelter.

'Who is it?' I repeated.

Her voice was high, tight, incredulous. 'My mama. She says *he's* there. He go my home.' Then she was scratching, scraping the wall again and speaking once more into the mouthpiece, her words shrill and anxious.

'What's going on?'

She spat a final, urgent command into the wavering

mobile, then raised her face. Her skin was paper-white, blanched. 'My mama she says he won't go. He want stay my home. She scared. She says he has no hair.'

'What about your father?'

'Not there. Drinking.'

'Well tell her to call the police.'

Sachiko shook her head. 'No, bad thing to call. I don't want. Everyone see.'

'Maybe Mr Kanazawa could help.'

Again she shook her head. 'He don't know.'

'About him?' It was as if I too could not bring myself to use his name. Unspoken, it flickered strangely beneath our words.

'No.'

'What's he doing anyway?'

'Nothing. Just sitting. My mama she scared . . . But where is his hair?'

'It's all gone,' I said. 'It's quite a sight.'

She resumed blurting instructions into the mouthpiece.

'Look,' I said. 'Tell Kanazawa your mother's ill. Say you need his car. I'll come with you.'

'I can't.' Her frustrated nails, once again, clawed the wall. Her thin eyes were wet. She lowered her head, momentarily emitting an odd, high-pitched moan.

'I'll wait for you downstairs.'

'The driver will tell.'

'Charm him,' I said. 'Use that special charm.'

'What's happening for godsake?' Vickers was standing behind me. 'Thank Christ Kanazawa's half deaf and still looking at that fucking sunset. What have you done to her?'

Sachiko ran from us, across the room, towards her stunted millionaire guardian. He turned, bemused, as he heard her calling, suddenly looking very old and alone as he stood there, blackly silhouetted against the cold but sumptuous unscrolled skyline which he'd helped to make. And then we all turned, guests hopeful and hosts fearful of a scandal.

# 17

## SCENES FROM THE EASTERN CAPITAL

I saw but couldn't hear Sachiko order the driver, leaning over him, the light from a street lamp momentarily striping her face, his uniformed shoulders, the high backs of the seats. He quietly braked where I stood at the underlit mouth of the cul-de-sac of garages behind Vickers's mansion block. I placed my hand on the passenger door. His eyes didn't stray from the road of flaring headlights immediately ahead as I fell into the leathery embrace of the back seat, Sachiko's thin body beside me.

'He's certainly changed,' I said, of Meadowlark.

Sachiko said nothing.

We sped through Roppongi. She continued to ignore me, crossing her arms and lowering her head, a posture I'd never seen her adopt before. Outside I glimpsed the familiar Friday night scene. White men in suits. Micro-skirted local girls. An old, solitary Japanese woman, mouth and nose masked by gauze, shuffling her stooped way between the bored Caucasian women, model-tall and model-thin, sowing their nightclub flyers. It was strange to think that buried deep beneath their stiletto heels, below the new city's concrete and macadam, hidden far under the feet of all the unaware, just released white men on heat, their wallets corpulent with yen, was an older, forgotten city of wood (long ago reduced to powder, ash and shards), a lost, labyrinthine world of wooden houses, wooden bridges, lanterns and silk-wrapped bodies. Then it was all behind us, uniform office buildings, faintly chequered down their tall sides by still lit windows, replacing the neon coquetry of Roppongi's streetlife like a sudden massing of grey-suited giants. We drove between these dour, brooding hulks stuffed with paper and circuitry.

Sachiko was making a call. She spoke briefly, calmly. I was surprised by this new-found composure.

'Is he still there?'

'Yes.'

'What's he doing?'

'Just sitting. And saying strange things.'

'Strange things?'

'Just strange things.' She was now sliding out her pink-wrapped organizer. I watched while she reached up to turn on the light. She knew this car, its features, well. One shining painted nail with its delicate adornment of petals flicked over the stiff pages. They were dense with writing and numbers. A loose inserted sheet, perforated like a set of stamps, caught my attention.

'Can I?' I said, and then pulled it out without waiting for her to object.

'No. Don't. Private.'

She snatched unsuccessfully at my intrusive hand. I brought the sheet up close to my eyes. It was a page of *print club* stickers, stamp-sized and identical, the same pair of tiny photographic heads superimposed sixteen times on the same baroque blue and purple background of rising, stylized waves and two leaping, uninterested dolphins positioned like miniature bookends. Sixteen Sachikos sweetly simpered beside sixteen goggling Mr Kanazawas (they'd had no such thing, none of these *print clubs*, when he was a young man on the make in the ruins of Tokyo), his cheeks ruddy with alcohol, no doubt being supported in the booth by an invisible Kumamoto's loyal hands.

'Nice,' I said, returning it.

'Private,' she said. 'Rude.'

'Does Mr Kanazawa like KoKo Wanabe also?'

'Of course,' she said. 'All my friends like KoKo Wanabe.' Then her call was answered and she was talking fast in Japanese, her voice urgent, adult, clotted with imperatives. Then, just as abruptly, it was finished. She switched off the light.

'Who was that?'

'Not your business.'

'No,' I conceded.

'You always want know not your business,' she continued, looking out of the window, her small eyes and nose and mouth reflected back at her with unforgiving clarity (as was my own face, behind her face). 'It's bad thing.'

'I know. Terrible.'

'I want go away,' she continued.

'Go away. Where?'

'Don't know.'

I studied her sour reflection. Sometimes she was beautiful but sometimes something was missing and that beauty became its opposite. Now something was missing. 'But this is your city. You're a rising star.'

She said nothing.

'Your guardian's a millionaire.'

I realized she was crying. Silently crying. I watched tears drip and glint their way down her dark, reflected face. We were passing through Ryogoku, an old district of the city where the sumo wrestlers (like KoKo Wanabe's bashfully smiling, mountainous boyfriend) trained in their stables. I saw to one side of us the outline of the stadium.

Sachiko wiped her eyes and sniffed but didn't sink back into the pungent leather of the seat. Steam-filled noodle shops, dubious bars, hanging lanterns the colour of coalfire, one small shrine with its *torii* gate, a huddle of gabled houses slipped across her dark, reflected face (and mine also, watching over her shoulder), all with an oil painting's glisten. I wondered what Meadowlark was doing now. Whether he was still merely sitting there, uttering *strange things*.

'Shouldn't you ring your mother?'

She didn't answer me.

We drove. Tokyo merged imperceptibly with its dreary dormitory towns whose lit-up tower blocks and gloomy lanes of houses fed it every day with working bodies.

Time passed. For a while the fairytale extravagance of Cinderella's Castle at Tokyo Disneyland was faintly visible on the horizon. Tokyo Disneyland (I knew) was deemed a *hot date*, although I'd no idea whether Meadowlark and Sachiko had ever spent a combustible afternoon there among the screams and the rides and the queues and the mashed ice-cream cones.

I glanced at Sachiko. She'd now slumped back in the seat and was staring fixedly ahead, apparently at the driver's stubbled nape, her expression remote and preoccupied. So I didn't ask whether she'd ever climbed (if that was what one did), hand in hand with her discarded giant, Cinderella's plastic castle.

I must have dozed for suddenly I became aware of Sachiko's voice, speaking not to me but once more into her phone, leaning forward as she did so, almost crouching, her expression now wary, cautious, calculating. We were slowing. We'd arrived.

Rising up to my left was a tall concrete block with two concrete wings, half the height of the main block, creating a floodlit forecourt filled with parked cars. I lifted my eyes, counting the floors. Walkways ran the length of each floor behind high, bleak parapets. Wondering if it might be Meadowlark, I followed the progress of a man along the walkway five floors up as he passed with an expedited stride each of the firmly closed, plain front doors with their small adjacent windows.

Not waiting for Mr Kanazawa's driver, Sachiko had already depressed the handle and slipped out. I followed her. She'd paused a few feet from the car and stood gazing up with raw, uncloaked hatred at the floodlit stack of silent passageways.

I followed her to the lift. The interior was bleak and functional, but clean. We rose to the sixth floor.

I followed her along the walkway, passing dismal door after dismal door. Cold night air chafed my face. Above and below us, to our left and right, nothing moved along the other walkways nor down in the forecourt of cars.

She stopped at the seventh or eighth door (I'd lost count by then) and scrabbled in the depths of her handbag. This went on for a while. She certainly kept the thing full. Finally she snapped it shut and stabbed at the lock.

We stepped into a tiny hallway, its floor six inches below the top of the step that led, past an inner door fractionally ajar, through to the shadowy interior. Obedient to the overarching dictates of custom, Sachiko bent to remove her shoes, so I did likewise. The flat beyond smelt strongly of soya sauce and boiled rice. It seemed as silent and deserted as the long walkways and floodlit forecourt outside. I noted, among the discarded pairs of shoes, that there were none large enough to contain a pair of big Caucasian feet.

We continued into the flat. I couldn't hear Meadowlark's voice (or anyone else's) uttering *strange things*. Immediately to my right was a small bedroom. A young boy sat with his back to the open door playing a computer game, his unmoving head and shoulders outlined by the glow of the terminal, the only source of light in that room. Odd, soft electronic sounds (muted cries and squawks, the impact of comic book blows, congratulatory bursts of synthesized music) emanated randomly as he pursued some dungeon-based quest. He didn't look round as we passed. He was probably at the very deepest level.

The next door was closed. Sachiko opened it. Again the only light issued from a screen, this time a television screen. Intermittently it clarified the face of a prone body, buried to its neck in blankets, on a thin, unrolled futon. The head didn't move but one eye, I'm sure, did. I smiled at Sachiko's grandfather. 'Good evening, sir,' I said, in Japanese. On the screen a samurai drama was in progress. An old man (though not as old as the room's watching, motionless occupant) with a full beard, hair white as a swan, was dispensing wisdom against a backdrop of spear-carriers. Those around him nodded appreciatively as they absorbed his fine words.

Sachiko closed the door. Just ahead of us were two enormous empty boots, scuffed and dirty, one lying on its side. We stared together at them, she barefoot, I in my socks. It was an ugly sight, certainly for Sachiko. Crusted footwear contemptuously abandoned after crossing the threshold which separated the world inside (her family's small, private world) from that outside. I pictured him pulling them off as a mocking afterthought in front of Sachiko's assembled family. Except that her father wasn't there and her grandfather lay on his back, swaddled like a baby or a corpse, unable to stand without assistance, and her brother, with the intuitive quickness of the adolescent young, was too busy penetrating the very deepest level of his dungeonquest.

Ahead of us was the kitchen door, also shut.

She stepped around, I over, the baleful presence of Meadowlark's boots (they reeked) and paused in front of it. Another bland, blank surface, painted the mildest buttercup. No, there was no exoticism here, in this ordinary space, to excite the jaded Westerner's senses. I made a gesture of invitation with my hand. But I could see her fear had returned, had muscled its way back into her face. So I pushed the door for her.

He was sitting at the kitchen table, torso, chest, shoulders bulging out of the skimpiest of T-shirts, thick forearms and vast, splayed hands placed flat in front of him. The T-shirt was stark white and carried, between the pectorals, one word in bold, complete with exclamation mark:

**HI!**

'Hello there,' I said.

He smiled at me, at us, now lazily scratching the very point which declared

## HI!

'Do you want some tea?' he asked us. 'Your mother,' he told Sachiko, 'is making me some tea.'

This was true. There was a Japanese woman in an apron (across which waddled the image of foolish, innocent Jemima Puddle-duck) standing uncertainly beside a tall jug kettle. She had a spade-shaped face, deeply scored, and thin dry hair. Only her eyes reminded me of Sachiko. Maybe the origin of Sachiko's beauty, I speculated, resided in her absent father.

Meadowlark, meanwhile, turned his shaven monk's head round to address Sachiko's mother.

'Make tea for everyone,' he told her in Japanese.

And Sachiko's mother began to fiddle nervously with the teapot. It was a traditional design, the handle a conical stump protruding from the curved side.

An odd smugness was there on Meadowlark's face, like a practitioner (I thought) of one-night stands proud to be surprised in the aftermath of a conquest, an *ippatsu yaro* (as the Japanese term it), a one-hit guy.

'I see you've made yourself at home,' I said.

'I've been showing her some photographs while we wait for Sachiko's father.' He looked at Sachiko. 'What happened to your hair?'

She didn't answer. She was trembling; vibrating like a generator in a way which promised, shortly, an explosion.

'It was a stupid thing to do,' I said. 'You shouldn't have come.'

'Why not? It was time someone did. If you must know,

I considered it my, well, my responsibility.' Once again he idly scratched at the spot which said **HI!** 'I'm sure neither of you ever thought I'd be able to find my own way here. Unaided. But as you can see—' He spread his arms, smiling. The braggadocio of the one-hit guy.

'It was a stupid thing to do,' I said again. 'You—'

'Here! Look!' And he threw them at us, photographs, not many. They fluttered quietly to the floor around the table. 'I've shown her them, Sachiko. She's seen them all. All of them. It's over now. Everything's over.'

'You sound like a cut-price prophet,' I said. And bent to pick up the nearest of the photographs. I noted, among other things, that Sachiko didn't Caucasianize her nipples.

And then Sachiko (now behind me) began to scream – scream words, that is, not simply sounds. Japanese words. At her mother. Maybe at Meadowlark also, if she believed he could understand. Certainly his Japanese seemed to be on the march. He'd moved to the head of the class, I was tempted to tell him.

Her mother listened. In downcast silence. Doubly shamed, I supposed: first by Meadowlark, now by this. Her expression – I thought – was typical for her generation – for a woman, that is, of her generation. Someone who understands (all too well usually) but does not know how to act. So, unable to act, unable now even to continue the familiar motions of tea-making, she simply stood there.

'You shouldn't have come,' I told him again. Even more the second time, my words sounded limp and pointless.

The one-hit guy scratched leisurely at his **HI!**

'You know, you should do something about that itch,' I said.

'Well, you seem to have an itch all over.' He scratched

and smiled, unperturbed by Sachiko's unrelenting tirade which continued like a storm around us.

But then, as storms do, it abated. The furious wine-splash mouth fell quiet. And for a moment mother and daughter were silent together, looking at each other. I say together because it was a silence that excluded Meadowlark and me and the scattered photographs. Meadowlark's eyes moved from one to the other. I realized he was enjoying himself, filling and dominating the room, so certain that he was bringing the truth back home.

'Let's go,' I said. 'You've done what you wanted to do. Let's go.'

'Uh uh.' He shook his shaven monk's head. 'Uh uh. I'm waiting for her father.'

'He's pissed in some bar. He won't be back for hours.'

'I can wait.' Meadowlark leaned forward, resting a reflective chin in his palm.

'I've told Sachiko to call the police.'

'Yes, but she won't will she?'

'Japanese prisons are nasty places. They beat you if you look the warders in the eye.'

'I'm sure you're right,' said Meadowlark. 'But she won't will she? Will you?' His gaze had settled again on Sachiko. 'Will you?'

She didn't answer.

'Where's this tea, then?' His head twisted back, turning on its neck the way a snake's head might, making Sachiko's mother start even before he'd repeated his question in Japanese.

'She's frightened of you,' I said.

'I know.' He smiled.

After looking once at her daughter in a way which I

couldn't decipher, Sachiko's mother resumed preparing tea, carefully, keeping her counsel, an adept of the closed mouth, the neutral gaze, lining up the handleless cups, quietly pouring, maintaining this unreal pretence of normality (despite the presence of the foreigner whose head turned like a snake's, despite the spring pictures of her only daughter scattered near her feet, despite the other foreigner whose presence had yet to be properly explained), quietly pouring while keeping her true thoughts buried deep beneath the harshly scored surface of her dipped, spade-shaped face.

We listened together to the gentle sounds this activity made.

But then the door whispered open behind us. I knew that from the sudden twitch of interest in Meadowlark's face and eyes.

'Hello there, young fellow,' said Meadowlark grandly in English.

I turned. Sachiko's twelve-year-old brother stood there, barefoot, in loose stonewashed jeans and a blood-red XL T-shirt that almost reached his knees, holding an empty glass in one hand.

'I want some water,' he explained quietly in Japanese. He was taller than Sachiko. He had her eyes.

'Hi,' said Meadowlark.

'Hi,' said the boy in the same soft voice.

Sachiko's mother came hurrying towards him, holding a fresh glass of water, trying to shoo and fuss her son from the kitchen, but he didn't want to go; he held his ground.

'Why is the man still here?' he asked (in Japanese).

Meadowlark smiled and made a beckoning gesture; he must have understood the question. It suddenly occurred to me that he wanted to show the boy the photographs.

'What are you trying to do? Destroy her family?'

'I'm trying to tell the truth,' said Meadowlark. And again he beckoned the boy, but Meadowlark's smile and the movement of his vast, bare arm must have intimidated Sachiko's brother, for he didn't move; simply stood there; those eyes, which were so like Sachiko's, riveted by Meadowlark's body, by that smiling face. Was he trying to imagine this foreigner embracing his sister's slight frame, enwrapping it as fully and ferociously as would an anaconda, winding its scaly self around her, coil after bulging coil, asphyxiating and consuming her? But perhaps he had no idea there was such a scene to be imagined. Or perhaps he imagined it of me, not of that body with the ascetic monk's head, but of my altogether punier form.

'Why is the man still here?' he asked again in Japanese. The mildness of his voice was, if anything, perplexing. Apart from his eyes there seemed nothing at all of Sachiko in him.

But then we heard a guttural shout, muted as it came to us from behind two doors.

'Hi, honey, I'm home,' said Meadowlark.

We waited for Sachiko's father to appear. He took his time, presumably unaware that he had guests – but then he must have seen my shoes and, beyond the sacred threshold, Meadowlark's, our unfamiliar footwear which would have put him on notice of our presence however much whisky or sake he'd drunk with his colleagues that evening, so perhaps that was the reason for the delay; he was bending, lifting up, inspecting with an expression poised somewhere between uncertainty and concern each discarded alien shoe in turn, maybe turning them over, considering their soles, noting what big feet the boldest of the two intruders had.

He came in. His bleak synthetic suit (perhaps bought at Taka-Q) and strong smell redolent of the bar (as if an invisible counter and stool had slid in with him), an odour compounded of alcohol and cigarette smoke, of the *mama-san* and her girls' trenchant perfume, would have pricked Professor Tokugawa's sympathetic interest. Perhaps the professor's wise words on conflict between the generations, on the disappearance of gratitude, of honour, of respect, would have consoled him. He looked like a man who might need consolation, this befuddled and fallen blasphemer, this unashamed enemy of fashion and style and the internationally recognized label who had run amok amongst his own daughter's painstakingly assembled collection (and had never afterwards, so far as I was aware, shown remorse).

He stood and gazed with utter incomprehension at Meadowlark and me. Clearly our discarded shoes had done nothing to prepare him for this reality he could touch of two *gaijin*, two foreign strangers, one huge and one not, in his own kitchen, the kitchen his unappreciated labour of twenty years had paid for.

'Good evening,' said Meadowlark in Japanese.

'Good evening,' said Sachiko's father, his voice flatter, dryer, more controlled than I'd expected. His face was strong-featured; there was a street-hardness to his mouth. I felt he was a man who might not necessarily enjoy paying obeisance to his superiors. In different circumstances, I thought, it would have been interesting to discuss his views of the social system obtaining here in his country, his observations on the role of hierarchies, of oligarchies both at work and in his wider world. He wasn't drunk, that was certain. For I knew that when drunk he became maudlin, having witnessed this at one remove months before in McDonald's (or had it been Mister Donut?) while he burbled to Sachiko from a public phone in his favourite bar, eyes perhaps on his empty whisky *bottle-keep* as the *chi-mama* plucked it up, mournfully wondering while he spoke to his only daughter if he could afford another to go up on the shelf in its place bearing his name, to be lifted down and brought over to him on each successive visit. No, he wasn't that, and I saw, or thought I saw, the same thought occurring to Meadowlark also; visible, quite suddenly, on the surface of his face, the realization that he, despite his size, was no longer entirely in control.

'Who are these people?' Sachiko's father asked his wife in Japanese. 'Why did you let them in?'

Watching and listening to him, I remembered – unexpectedly – an anecdote from Sachiko's childhood, a rare memory confided by her to Meadowlark (and by him to me, back in the early days), of how as she tried, as a sweet child, to master her *hashi*, her chopsticks, fumbling the things, still inexpert, clumsy as she sought to eat her rice at family mealtimes, her father would lean across her mother and roughly grab her little hand between his own chopsticks, tightly pincering the soft flesh, annoyed at her childish ineptitude (after so much parental coaching, so much practice), angrily asking her, 'Aren't you Japanese, eh? Aren't you Japanese?' while roughly shaking that little trapped hand between the rigid compass of his *hashi*. I looked at Sachiko. From her expression she could have been remembering the very same thing.

But even as his wife started to talk to him in a low, tired voice, too low for me to even try to understand, he turned away from her and bent to pick up the nearest of the spring pictures.

Sachiko rushed at him with a frightened shriek, trying to rip it from his hand, but he was too strong. Easily restraining her with one arm, he considered the photograph, taking his time. His eyebrows were dark and very straight. His eyes gave no clues to his thoughts regarding this image he was contemplating. It could have been some art work quite irrelevant to his life.

While Sachiko stood there, sobbing into her hands (all I could see now was her fashionably roughened, auburn-lightened hair, of which she must have been so proud when she first emerged into the sunlight wearing it), her father abruptly crumpled the picture to a dense ball in his hand. Now he was looking (most grimly) at Meadowlark.

## ALL THAT IS LEFT OF THE WARRIORS' DREAM

Perhaps Meadowlark had hoped to find common ground between them, since he too was now an enemy, equally unashamed, of the internationally recognized label and all that it signified. But he was given no opportunity to move towards this common ground – if it existed – for Sachiko's father, with a shout or grunt I couldn't interpret, swatted him with full palm and fingers across the face, and then again, and again. Meadowlark rose, hugely but unsteadily, taken aback, pushing out while shielding his eyes. Showing the unanticipated canniness of a street fighter, Sachiko's father turned away, looking for some weapon with which to secure an unfair advantage. Back round he swung, now holding a saucepan. It seemed a curiously domestic, even feminine choice of hardware. With a fusillade of bestial grunts he managed to land two blows before Meadowlark caught his wrist and held it.

'Don't you think we should leave?' I said to Meadowlark. He turned his flushed face to me.

'I'm going to talk to him. Tell him I'm *going* to talk to him.'

Sachiko's father was trying unsuccessfully to snap free from the foreigner's steel grip, emitting his grunts now with the rapidity of a machine-gun as he discovered that he was not, perhaps, as strong as he'd thought.

'You tell him. You seem to have mastered the language.'

Sachiko's father, with a final, extended grunt, broke Meadowlark's hold. He now withdrew a couple of steps, and ordered his family to quit the kitchen. No one moved. He shouted at them to go.

'That's a pretty mean saucepan,' I said. 'And I reckon he's used it before. I think you should leave.'

'Shut up, fake.' Meadowlark was wiping at the sweat on his face. As if he needed to be clean and dry in order to fight.

'Fake?' I said.

'Fake, fake, fake,' he began to repeat as he rubbed one eye with a knuckle – lifting his spectacles' frame as he did – and then the other. He could have been ridding them of congealed sleep. 'That's what I said. *Fake.*'

'I think I get the point you're trying to make.'

Once again Sachiko's father raised his guttural voice, trying to clear the kitchen for further combat. His son hesitated; he appeared to be about to move. But that was all. Neither Sachiko nor her mother wavered.

Sachiko's father began to shout. As far as I could ascertain (for he spoke rapidly, abusively) he was blaming his wife for allowing in this stranger, this alien, this, this (he groped for the appropriate words) enormous pig, and also Sachiko – for everything, for this, this (once again he groped but this time unsuccessfully for an all-encompassing noun) – for the absence of all respect or concord or duty in their home which his labours alone made possible.

And then, once more, he flourished the saucepan.

Meadowlark, for protection, now lifted the nearest kitchen chair.

'Who were the other girls?' I asked him. 'I found the photographs.'

He didn't turn. He wasn't distracted. 'Just sluts . . . Like her.'

There was a telephone behind me, fixed to the wall. I lifted off the receiver and took out my wallet. I found the number I wanted. I started to dial.

Sachiko's father turned, his face stretched by disbelief. 'That is my telephone,' he said in incredulous Japanese. 'That is *my* telephone.'

My call was answered. An elderly man barked in English, his voice clearer and stronger than I'd expected, '*Yes?*' He sounded angry. (Congenitally not temporarily angry.)

'Good morning,' I told him. Which it was, where he was standing, probably just after dawn. Clearly he was an early riser. I swung round to face Meadowlark, proffering the receiver. 'Would you like to say something? It's your father.'

'*Hello? Hello?*' his father kept repeating, already

exasperated by my inefficiency. '*Who is this? I said who is this? Hello? . . . Hello?*'

'Don't you want to speak to him?'

'*Will whoever this is—*'

'Why don't you—'

Meadowlark was staring at me.

With a great and warlike cry, Sachiko's father brought the saucepan hurtling round to connect with the back of his head.

'*I said will whoever this is—*'

I replaced the receiver, leaving Meadowlark's father alone with his annoyance and an insoluble mystery. That would gall him. A damn, infuriating mystery (and so early in the morning).

When I finally intervened, stepping between them, Meadowlark had fallen to his knees, hunching and covering his head. There was blood bright and dark between his fingers.

I don't know at what point Sachiko's father would have stopped if I hadn't, for the rage which was driving him on now seemed to exceed the events of that evening. He was no longer just striking out at one invasive, monstrous foreigner. Whatever his true target, it transcended that. I could see it in his eyes, in the odd locking of his face, as I held his trembling forearms, telling him in Japanese (as I felt the strength and anger coursing beneath the skin, stubborn and unappeased), 'You mustn't. You mustn't.'

He strained against me.

'You mustn't. You mustn't.'

Meadowlark moaned, still on his knees, still grasping his bowed head in his hands.

'You mustn't. Please. You mustn't.'

## 18

## STARS OF THE NIGHTLESS CITY

It was past midnight, about a month later; I was shopping in the twenty-four-hour 7–Eleven in Roppongi, walking along the stainless steel aisles, feeling less and less hungry as I shuffled among packets of rice crackers and instant noodles under the unsparing fluorescence. I extracted a can of soft drink from the refrigerator; peered through the cold transparent casing of the remaining ready-to-eat meals with their little plastic vials of soya sauce and recessed compartments of tired rice, breadcrumbed chicken and nastily bright pink and yellow pickles. My slow, listless passage eventually brought me back to the magazine rack placed up against the window. There was the usual slick panoply of periodicals and the ubiquitous browsing teenage boy, acne a vivid crimson in that platinum light, who'd just finished scrutinizing various swollen, gleaming motorbikes and had now moved on to looking at naked bodies.

As I moved alongside him he turned a page and naked bodies gave way to clothed ones. Amongst a jumble of captioned photographs – assorted celebrities framed from unexpected angles, generously bestowing their aura on the neon nightless city of Tokyo – was one of . . . *Sachiko.* I gawped. Or at least I thought it was Sachiko – she was concealed by heavy shades; yes, I was sure it was Sachiko, and wearing (in the dead of night) shades, maybe all that midnight neon hurt her eyes, maybe they made her feel sexy and mysterious, even while bumping into things, I don't know – but I was sure – and then once again I wasn't so sure; if it was her, she was nimbly exiting a stretched limousine, hanging on the arm of her escort, a gangling man throttled by black leather with spectacular badger hair that fringed his waist. I knew from late-night videos watched while sprawled on the sofa in my darkened flat that this was the lead singer of Black Kettle, no less, those big-hitting, hard-drinking glam rockers from Osaka. I even remembered his name. 'Mick' Murayama. He was twenty-six. Only the slimmest oval of face was visible through his lustrous haystack of hair.

I drew out another copy of the same magazine to verify my sighting. I found the page of naked bodies and then the jumbled spread of captioned photographs, the same celebrities caught from the same odd angles, bestowing with equal, indifferent munificence their gorgeous aura on the nightless city. It was certainly Sachiko. She'd struck oil this time. Black Kettle – in their thigh-high boots, their rhinestone codpieces, their waist-length badger hair – presently bestrode the world of Japanese rock. I wondered what had happened to Mr Kanazawa, who was not a person to upset. Perhaps he had smiled on the union.

I didn't buy the magazine. I wasn't that interested. Instead I went home to crunch my way through my packet of rice crackers and drink my soft drink. It was 1 a.m. For the fifth, or sixth, or seventh successive night (I'd long ago lost count) I sprawled on the sofa in my darkened flat (the numberless lights of Tokyo outside my high-rise window, a spectacle I equally loved and feared) and let the TV's blaze – for was it not the late John Lennon who so percipiently likened its silent background presence to that of a lit fireplace's comforting glow and movement? – let its blaze dance and occupy my tired eyes, tired by too many words squeezed too close together on too many sheets of paper . . . At first I thought I was dreaming, but in fact I was only part-dreaming and – yes – 'Mick' Murayama and the rest of Black Kettle were indeed grinding their dissolute codpieces against the screen of my TV as if they wanted to burst out into the living-room and pelvically thrust their way around my sofa. I couldn't find the remote. I ran at the TV to turn it black.

Thereafter, for weeks, I seemed unable to turn without seeing her (at one remove, in photographic form), seductively peeking over a swaying salaryman's shoulder on the underground from his wilting broadsheet, grasped between the hands of my sullen young neighbour at the counter of a sushi bar, at ease and in full colour in the magazine rack at 7–Eleven. I felt I was being haunted, seized by some cheap, low-level delirium. (Meadowlark, at least, had had the good grace to have no media rebirth. He'd left, taking his image with him.) Yet on and on it went, this ridiculous haunting. Lesser characters, bit-part players, also made an appearance – I saw Professor Tokugawa, inexplicably, on a sports page (benignly chuckling, of course) and Mr Kanazawa (in grumpy, grainy monochrome) being sheltered by Kumamoto's umbrella in one corner of a pull-out supplement on kabuki and modern dance. But principally it was Sachiko's ghost which pursued me, always accompanied by 'Mick', indefatigable foghorn voice of those big-hitting, badger-haired glam rockers from

Osaka, the two of them invariably giving the greedy lenses Churchillian reverse V-signs – jointly V-signing as they got into taxis and limousines, jointly V-signing as they got out, V-signing at a celebrity party, at an album launch in Ginza, even giving their flamboyant Churchillians on the way to his grandmother's ninetieth birthday. Sometimes, perhaps for variety, the lead singer of Black Kettle just pointed with a forefinger at his head, Sachiko triumphantly V-signing beside him.

As for Meadowlark, according to one reliable source he'd left for Thailand. Another, rival reliable source placed him in the Philippines. Sometimes he was said to be living the life of a rigorous ascetic, sometimes that of a disinhibited libertine. A duller alternative claim was that he was back in England, living with his parents, stooping to fit in under the ceiling of their retirement bungalow, idling away the time which now stretched coldly ahead of him, as if he too were retired.

# PART THREE

# 19

## BEAUTIFUL TREE, BROKEN BRIDGE

At the age of eighteen (he was now twenty-five) Bunji had spent the months of July, August and September in England, boarding with a local family in a village just outside Newquay. He'd developed a taste for the English countryside and the conservative fabric of the life he'd found there. Indeed, for a long time after his return he could talk of little else, broaching his experiences at every opportunity until this habit, diverting at first, had become an established family joke, laughingly referred to by the others as Bunji's 'English disease'.

Now he built wooden houses in the old style. But there were too many people on this archipelago of islands (millions and millions of them, all with their own aspirations, their own dreams, millions upon millions of aspirations and dreams) and never enough land, never enough wood, even though there were logging companies hard at work, year in, year out, decimating the tropical forests of Sarawak and Borneo. So Bunji's future, whatever his private leanings, could only ever be one of building for the rich, for the few. Still, that did not stop him looking in his work for some larger moral and, as we sat together one warm spring afternoon, admiring the great incomplete structures of the houses he and his *sensei* were building in Nara among trees laden with cherry blossom, he talked of a time – he didn't say when but he talked as if it were possible – when all Japan might return to living in wooden houses, built like these in the old style. He took the long view. As to whether the present frantic manufacturing and money-making, for decades so successful, would last; maybe (he speculated) the crazed neon of Ginza and Roppongi would wink one final time – and go out. Go dark. Maybe the white men in suits, their profits evaporating, would pack up their dealing rooms and go home. (And, briefly, I imagined the women's army of 1945 that never was, Yumie and her dead mother and millions like them, surging with their sharpened bamboo staves through the clubs and bars of night-time Roppongi, startling, scattering Harvey and his friends, commencing a primitive onslaught which would take them even as far as the red-glazed streets and pleasure stores – with their waiting passive nutbrown girls – of Bangkok and Phuket.)

So Bunji took the long view, but it seemed unlikely. I knew that true simplicity was not attainable anymore. I thought of Meadowlark – whatever had become of him. I thought of Sachiko. I hadn't seen her for a long time, other than in photographs, although I had seen many girls like her, chewing gum, sullen, bored, drifting through the streets of Roppongi, along the wide pavements of Omotesando Avenue. Sachiko and Meadowlark: minor links in a long chain of fantasy and abuse. But Bunji insisted, as we sat there admiring his half-built houses and the delicate blossom, that nothing was permanent and therefore anything was possible. He banged with his cane for emphasis on the ground. I noticed there were crumbs of shortbread (sent to him from England by my amused, intrigued mother) on his lower lip. His cream blazer rested on his knees, so I could admire his light cream waistcoat and silk tie. All that was missing was a straw boater. Of course he was ridiculous, risible, sitting there in a waistcoat, looking forward to a time of eighteenth-century houses and street scenes like an Edo print come to life. He was my friend, but I could still see him for what he was. And yet, I thought, in his waistcoated, carefully combed, eau-de-cologned ridiculousness, there was also something faintly heroic. Bunji stood.

And, without a word, started walking, and so I followed. Towards the bare, upright skeletons, palely flecked with dislodged blossom, of his half-completed wooden houses.

4-28-21